FARMING
AND
DEMOCRACY

By
A. WHITNEY GRISWOLD

This lively book questions one of the sturdiest dogmas of the American political faith — the belief that the independent farmer tilling his own land is "the backbone of democracy." This belief, at least professed by nearly every political leader since Thomas Jefferson, has been the basis of a vast governmental system of aid to the farmer which, together with the present worldwide food shortage, has put the American farmer at a peak of prosperity. Can that prosperity last? Is the political theory that buttresses it a sound one?

Mr. Griswold tests the theory by tracing the history of farming and democratic progress over the past century and a half in the three great western democracies — Great Britain, France, and the United States. His conclusions will be surprising: that British democracy made its greatest forward strides during a period when the owner-operated small farm was practically disappearing from the landscape, and that French democracy has survived despite the influence of the small French proprietor. Only in the United States can some sort of case be made for family farming as a mainstay of democracy, and the evidence today is that the old-fashioned type of family farm is a poor economic risk for the long run as well as a poor bulwark for the defense of democratic institutions. What the American farmer needs, says Mr. Griswold in a concluding chapter, is not a government subsidy for his vote as a "free American," but a realistic replanning of American farming to fit the needs and receive the full benefits of twentieth century democracy.

Farming and Democracy

By the Same Author

THE FAR EASTERN POLICY OF THE UNITED STATES

A. WHITNEY GRISWOLD

Farming and Democracy

NEW YORK

HARCOURT, BRACE AND COMPANY

To M. B. G.

"For the best material of democracy is an agricultural population; there is no difficulty in forming a democracy where the mass of the people live by agriculture or the tending of cattle."

Aristotle, *Politics*, *circa* 347 B.C.

". . . I have always considered the farmers of this country as the backbone of American democracy."

Representative August H. Andresen (Minnesota),
House of Representatives, 1947 A.D.

Preface

THIS IS a book about an idea—that farming as a family enterprise is the "backbone of democracy." The book discusses the origin of the idea, its historic influence on public policy in Great Britain, France, and the United States, and its possible significance for the future of both American agriculture and American democracy.

Questions concerning democracy are in the air these days. But the reader may wonder why the book should dwell on the troubles of our farmers just as they are enjoying the greatest boom in their history. When the New Deal measures described in the following pages went into effect, total farm income stood at $7,055,000,000. In 1940 it was $10,-965,000,000. Since then it has risen to nearly $30,000,000,-000. The current index of food prices is 286 per cent of its 1909-14 average, 22 per cent higher than the high following the First World War. With such figures as these in mind citizens who are not farmers may find it hard to conceive of farmers as the victims of chronic adversity.

The Second World War created a forced draft under American agricultural production, and the demands of a hungry world have kept it drawing. Department of Agriculture experts predict that it may continue to draw for another two or three years. No one can say exactly what the consequences would be, to our farmers or anyone else, if the present level of production and employment should be sustained indefinitely. These possibilities should not, however, blind us to the long-run trends described in these pages. While per capita net income to persons on farms has risen from $177 in 1940 to $620 in 1946, per capita net income to persons not on farms has risen from $721 to $1,326. In other words, instead of making nearly five times as much as the average farmer, the average non-farmer now makes only a little over twice as much. Moreover, these figures leave in dispute the idea (more popular in the city than on the farm) that compensating factors peculiar to the farmer's way of life make up the difference. The same sources that document the agricultural boom document a rural disadvantage in living standards and cultural opportunities—in housing, medical and health facilities, schools, and libraries—even greater than the disparity of income. These things are as much the essence of the farmer's way of life as his independence and his landscapes. The boom has not yet made good to him the democratic promise of equal opportunity in either the economic or the cultural sphere.

At the moment we are dedicated to a goal that promises equal opportunity to everybody—full production and employment in a free society—the highest possible efficiency in utilizing our economic resources within a political framework that preserves the highest possible degree of individual initiative, self-discipline, and self-improvement. We have declared these latter factors to be commensurate with economic efficiency. If farmers are to realize the full measure of either, it is more than likely that many will have to give up farming for employment in other industries. In the final analysis, much more is at stake in our attainment of that goal than the welfare of our farmers or of any other particular group—as much, conceivably, as the peace of the world and the future of democracy as a political system. It is in the hope of shedding some light upon these larger prospects that I submit this commentary on the democratic construction placed upon farming by the three countries which have taken the lead in interpreting democracy to the modern world.

For the opportunity to write this book I am indebted to the John Simon Guggenheim Memorial Foundation for a Fellowship I held in 1942 and 1945; to the Social Science Research Council for a Demobilization Award in 1945-46; and to Yale University, which gave me leave of absence to undertake the work. I am grateful to the Librarian and staff of the Yale University Library for many kindnesses; to the editor of the *American Political Science Review* for permission to incorporate parts of Chapter Two that had previously appeared in the *Review*; and to the following publications and publishers for permission to quote from works of their imprint: *Journal of Farm Economics* for "Schisms in Agricultural Policy" by Mordecai Ezekiel; The Clarendon Press, Oxford, for *The Enclosure and Redistribution of Our Land* by W. H. R. Curtler; *Economic History Review* for "Observations on the Open Fields" by C. S. Orwin; Longmans, Green and Company for *English Social History* by G. M. Trevelyan, and for *Land Reform* by J. Collings; Oxford University Press for *Country Planning* by The Agricultural Economic Research Institute of Oxford University; *Revue d'Economie Politique* for "Vingt-cinq Ans Dans la Structure Agricole Française" by M. Augé-Laribé; F. Lenig for *Questions Agraires aux Temps de la Terreur* by G. Lefèbvre; The Viking Press for *Grapes of Wrath* by John Steinbeck.

A. WHITNEY GRISWOLD

New Haven, Conn.
November 20, 1947

Contents

Farming and Democracy

CHAPTER ONE

Introduction

EVERY TURN of events, these days, puts to test the fundamental principles of democracy. "Political theory,"
Lord Lindsay tells us in *The Modern Democratic State*,[1]
"begins when, in some concrete situation, men begin arguing
that the nature of the state requires that some sort of action
should be or should not be taken." Everywhere, today, men
are arguing from theoretical assumptions concerning the nature of the state to practical conclusions of law and policy.
We cannot keep out of the argument. We have not kept out
of it. The greater the economic responsibilities we impose
upon the state, the more we are obliged to define the political
principles according to which those responsibilities shall be
discharged. The more determined our support for democracy
abroad, the more necessary it is for us to practice what we
preach at home. The barriers separating the practical politics
from the political theory of American democracy are down:
there is no significant instance of the one that is not a direct
extension and a test of the other.

We have steeped ourselves so thoroughly in the practical
and the empirical that we take to political theory with reluc-
tance. We do not like to reason things out in advance. We
would rather meet situations as they arise and dispose of
them with a domestic blend of precedent and rule of thumb.
But the situations we now judge vital to our national welfare
will not "arise." They will have to be induced; and since
democracy draws no distinction between ends and means, if

1. Vol. I, London, 1943, p. 31.

they are to conform with democratic ends they will have to be induced by democratic means. The whole prospect calls for meticulous attention to first principles every step of the way. We can no longer afford to say one thing and do another, to talk free enterprise and tolerate monopoly, to maintain an anti-trust law on our books and provide more ways of evading than of enforcing it. This is worse than inconsistency. It is an admission of failure that is already being used against democracy with telling effect by its critics and enemies. We can no longer indulge in the cynicism that interprets first principles as myths or ideologies. The opening sentences of Bulfinch's *Mythology* show us the end of that trail: "The religions of ancient Greece and Rome are extinct. The so-called divinities of Olympus have not a single worshipper among living men." If democracy is to survive we must believe in it, not as myth but as reality; and if we believe in it as reality we can hold no theoretical proposition of democracy too lightly to consider it as fact.

One such proposition, that has for some time been taken for granted in the United States and has recently found expression in the debate over political theory to which Lord Lindsay alludes, concerns the relationship between the agrarian and the democratic way of life. Of late, men have been arguing that the nature of the American state requires the preservation of the small, owner-operated, family-size farm. The argument brings into focus the general idea that the fate of democracy is somehow or other bound up with the fate of the agricultural community whence it emerged and that both may be sinking in an industrialized, collectivistic wave of the future. For the past ten years, this proposition has been receiving steadily increasing attention in the formulation and conduct of our national agricultural policy. It is this proposition that we propose to take seriously, even literally, in the following pages; to look into its historical origins and at the role it has played in the democratic countries whose economic and political experiences have foreshadowed or paralleled our own.

It is no concession to mythology to recognize the popularity of the family farm as a symbol of the good life in the United States. Plato says the ideal forms of human institutions are laid away in heaven; but this one is not. It is the daydream of city-dwellers, the inspiration of poets and artists, the biographer's security for the youth of great men. It stands for democracy in its purest and most classic form. For millions of Americans it represents a better world, past but not quite lost, one to which they may still look for individual happiness or, maybe, national salvation.

The romantic appeal of the symbol contrasts strangely with the economic fortunes of the reality. The years have not dealt kindly with the family farm. Once the home and livelihood of nine-tenths of the American people, it is now the home of less than a fifth of them and affords employment to barely 15 per cent of the working population. It is a home, moreover, that has been slipping from its owners' grasp. Nearly 40 per cent of the nation's farms were mortgaged in 1940 and an equal proportion leased. "For the past 55 years, the entire period for which we have statistics on land tenure, there has been a continuous and marked decrease in the proportion of operating owners and an accompanying increase in the proportion of tenants," a Presidential committee on farm tenancy reported in 1937.

Tenancy has increased from 25 per cent of all farmers in 1880 to 42 per cent in 1935. Because of debt the actual equity of operating owners is far less than these figures indicate. In some of our States, among them a number settled under the homestead system little more than a generation ago, it is estimated that the equity of operating farmers in their lands is little more than one-fifth. Nearly four-fifths is in the hands of landlords and mortgage holders.[2]

Conditions of life and labor among the rural population, of hunger, unemployment, ill health, poor education, inadequate housing, and general insecurity had begun to trouble the national conscience. There was an obvious discrepancy between the ideal and the real.

Most Americans were conscious of the discrepancy without being able to explain it. For the explanation lay in the, to them, still esoteric realm of economics. Moreover, the explanation conflicted with a long-held belief that the size and prosperity of the agricultural population were the most accurate measures of a nation's economic welfare. Actually, farming still occupied two-thirds of the earth's people. But in certain countries which had passed through the industrial revolution, or were in the process of passing through it, the agrarian ranks had been retreating before those of industry and commerce. The United States, England, Germany, Switzerland, Austria, Holland, Belgium, and Australia had passed the milestone beyond which the people employed in industry outnumbered those in agriculture.[3] Other nations were on the way. In all of these the size, and in most the relative prosperity, of the farm population showed a steady decline. The fundamental reason for this was that whereas the demand for industrial products was practically unlimited, the demand for agricultural products was not. There is a physiological limit to the volume of food consumption, and the demand for it, as compared with that for other goods, is closely linked to the level of population and of national income. Hence, the greater the expansion of the national income through industrialization, the smaller the portion of it received by farmers.

2. *Farm Tenancy*, Report of the President's Committee, 1937, p. 3.
3. See International Labour Office, *Year Book of Labour Statistics, 1941*, pp. 6-18.

In the United States, food constitutes between 80 and 90 per cent of the entire agricultural output, and the per capita consumption of food has remained surprisingly stable for the past forty years.[4] Thus, while the population increased 75 per cent (from 1899 to 1939) and industrial production 400 per cent, agricultural production increased only 50 per cent; and while the share of manufacturing in the national income rose from 19 to 30 per cent, the share of agriculture sank from 21 to 12 per cent.[5]

Foreign trade and industrial consumption, the two obvious substitutes for eating more food at home, have proved no exceptions to this rule. Hungry people in the overcrowded agrarian countries like China and India found no way to pay for agricultural imports from countries like the United States. Most of the industrialized countries were food importers, for whose markets the United States was driven into severe competition by Australia, Canada, New Zealand, Argentina, and Denmark. For military reasons and in the supposed interest of her own farm population, Germany barricaded herself behind agricultural tariffs. So did France. As competition increased and foreign markets dwindled, American producers of the great export crops, once free traders, turned protectionist and closed their own outlets. Nor could improvement in the national diet or domestic industrial consumption take up the slack. While the national diet has improved, especially during the recent sharp rise in employment and income, the change has not been sufficient to balance the trend; and for every agricultural product for which industry found use, science discovered a competitive non-agricultural prod-

4. For statistics, cf. Tolley, Howard R., "An Appraisal of the National Interest in the Agricultural Situation," *American Economic Review:* Papers and Proceedings, 1940, pp. 112-113; Barger, Harold, and Landsberg, Hans H., *American Agriculture, 1899-1939*, New York, 1942, Ch. IV.

5. Barger and Landsberg, *op. cit.*, pp. 19-25, 297.

uct. Meanwhile, agricultural machinery and technology, applied on a constantly expanding scale, increased the productive capacity of agriculture, depressing prices and wages, creating a labor surplus, and accelerating the flight from the land. The industrial revolution enabled a smaller farm population to produce more and better food for a larger total population, releasing workers from agriculture for relatively more productive employment in industry. Many moved with the trend; too many chose to resist it.

These were the true causes of the distress of agriculture and the decline of the farm population in the United States and the other industrialized countries during the past few decades, the basic explanation of the plight of the family farm. The fact was, there were too many farmers in relation to rapidly improving productive techniques and a relatively fixed demand for food. Their aggregate income would have to be spread too thin for all of them to prosper. But they did not see things this way. They did not understand their troubles as inevitable results of the industrial revolution. They did not comprehend them in charts and graphs. What they noticed were falling prices, unmarketable surpluses, rising costs of living, high rents and interest rates—symptoms, not causes. They saw the wealth and population of the country increasing while the profitableness of farming as a business enterprise declined, and they demanded treatment of the symptoms. They demanded protection against the impact of the industrial revolution on agriculture, preferring to make the best of their own *status quo*—as farmers—rather than to participate in any other way in the economic progress of the nation as a whole.

So it was that the rugged individualist of American tradition entered politics and became one of the principal beneficiaries of government support. He asked and received economic aid on an unprecedented scale. Basic crop prices, calculated as of the period of their maximum purchasing power (in some cases 1910 to 1914, in others, 1919 to 1929), were guaranteed by subsidy and endorsed by both parties under the slogan of "parity." An elaborate program of public credit, crop insurance, marketing controls, tariffs and import quotas, rural electrification, soil conservation, and technical assistance was undertaken by the government. The immediate purpose of all this governmental activity, which conformed to a fairly uniform pattern throughout the industrial countries, has been well stated by a former member of the British Ministry of Agriculture and Fisheries: ". . . the history of agriculture during the last twenty years is, in the main, the history of the various attempts made by ingenious politicians and civil servants to raise agricultural prices, or to keep them from falling, or to compensate the farmer for their fall, without attracting too much notice from the consumer—who pays either *qua* consumer or *qua* taxpayer." [6] Like the British, the American consumer pays so much for his bread and meat, plus so much more for public assistance to the farm population. The cost of this public assistance in all its manifold forms is not inconsiderable. In 1940, before the tremendous war spending began, it amounted to $1,416,122,000, the largest item of expense incurred by the federal government, including the individual (though not the combined) expenditures for the Army and Navy.[7] The total cost of food purchased by American consumers in 1935-1936 was about $14,500,000,000.[8] *Qua* consumers, *qua* taxpayers, or both,

6. Dale, H. E., "Agriculture and the Civil Service," in *Agriculture in the Twentieth Century*, Oxford, 1939, p. 15.

7. It was exceeded by the Independent Offices item, but this included such diverse activities as WPA, PWA, Social Security, TVA, Veterans Administration, etc. Total expenditures were $9,665,086,-000. See Dept. of Commerce, *Statistical Abstract of the U.S., 1941*, pp. 188-189.

8. *Ibid.*, 1943, p. 397.

they were paying a 10 per cent excise on their food in sub-
vention of existing methods of producing it and the social
institutions surrounding them. *Qua* consumers, they were
paying as much more as the amount added to the price of
food by the various forms of government intervention.

The average American is unaware of this hidden cost as he
buys his bread or pays his taxes. He may or may not appre-
ciate its political significance as a special concession to a particular economic group, according to whether or not he is
himself a farmer or has business with farmers. Strict cost ac-
counting would include the markup as overhead in the nation's food budget, and not just economic overhead. If the
machines, techniques, and scientific methods at present available were applied to agriculture with regard only to maximum production at minimum cost, it is probable that we
could maintain and even increase our food supply with half
the existing farm population.[9] The possibility is indicated by
what happened during the Second World War. From 1939
to 1945 we increased our production of crops 30 per cent,
and of livestock 40 per cent, in the face of a net reduction in
the farm population of 5,000,000 (15 per cent) and specific
losses to war industries and the armed forces of 40 per cent
of the male workers between fourteen and twenty-four and
over 20 per cent of those between twenty-five and forty-
four.[10]

The full productive capacity of American agriculture has
never been realized. Before the war 85 per cent of our food
was produced by half of our six million farms. As a leading
economist in the Department of Agriculture has put it, "The

9. Cf. Tolley, *loc. cit.*, p. 111; Yates, P. Lamartine, *Food Production in Western Europe*, London, 1940, p. 17.

10. Bureau of Agricultural Economics, U.S. Department of Agriculture, *The Agricultural Situation*, October, 1945, p. 8, and November, 1945, p. 47.

purchase of the least productive quarter of our farms, and their conversion to forest, might be fully counterbalanced by a good rain in the Corn Belt." [11] In 1937 over 1,500,000 men living on farms were counted as fully or partially unemployed,[12] and 600,000 families were on relief.[13] The average American farm is considerably larger and not nearly so intensively cultivated as the European, its yield per acre much lower. The effect of technology in reducing farm populations has been universally demonstrated and recognized.[14] Under such circumstances as these, the prediction that unlimited application of technology for maximum production would result in a 50 per cent reduction of the farm population seems conservative. "Full employment in agriculture is not just around the corner," two members of the Bureau of Agricultural Economics warned soon after the end of the war.

It will take many years of progressive adjustments of farm population to agricultural resources with corresponding changes in the size and organization of farming units. Since the total volume of agricultural production in the foreseeable future is subject to certain upper limits imposed both by total land resources and by demand for farm products, the total number of persons who can be employed in agriculture with adequate net returns for their labor is far smaller than the present number.[15]

The nation had emerged from the war committed to the principle of full employment. Few economists would differ

11. Baker, O. E., in Baker, Borsodi, Ralph, and Wilson, M. L., *Agriculture in Modern Life*, New York, 1939, p. 62.
12. Meyers, A. L., *Agriculture and the National Economy*, Temporary National Economic Committee Monograph No. 23, p. 5.
13. Tolley, *loc. cit.*, p. 115. This was in 1935-6.
14. Cf. U.S. Department of Agriculture, *Changing Technology and Employment in Agriculture*, 1941; Barger and Landsberg, *op. cit.*, Chs. V-VIII.
15. Ducoff, L. J., and Hagood, M. J., "Full Employment in Agriculture," *The Agricultural Situation*, October, 1945, pp. 11-12.

with this statement of the implications of that principle to agriculture.

Reduction of the farm population has proved itself a corollary to economic progress in all of the industrialized or partially industrialized countries. With the unproductive portion of the American farm population otherwise employed, the total agricultural income would go further among the remainder. If this reallocation of labor resources between agriculture and other enterprises were accompanied by a reallocation of productive resources within agriculture, subsidies to the latter might be greatly reduced. It might be necessary to continue national expenditures for such purposes as agricultural education, soil conservation, scientific research, and economic planning, but large sums spent every year in support of agricultural prices might be saved. Nor can the saving be calculated solely in terms of money. The persons who left farming should be able to find better economic and social opportunities than they could possibly find as farmers. The price of food might be reduced to the consumer and further improvements in the national diet effected, with such social benefits as may be surmised from the fact that millions of the supposedly well-fed citizens of the United States are victims of malnutrition. Agricultural tariffs might be removed and the way opened for a more profitable participation in the world market and the international economic organizations, the success of which is vital to the political organization of security and world peace. The national interest might be promoted in a variety of ways by the more effective utilization of resources and the more equable distribution of economic opportunity.

So far these possibilities—and that is all they are—have been realized only in the minds of economists. They have not penetrated the realm of practical politics, and for good reason. Farmers have opposed them, and so has the general public,

whose occasional outbursts against the "farm bloc" are tempered by feelings of sympathy for the rural population and
the agrarian way of life. It is not surprising in a nation whose
political affairs are increasingly dominated by a number of
powerful pressure groups, representing particular economic
and social interests, that the farmers have organized in this
manner. Although they differ sharply among themselves, and
the number and diversity of their organizations belie the
legend of a single unified bloc, the general tendency of all of
them is to maintain the *status quo* in American agriculture.
Cotton growers want to continue growing cotton; tobacco
growers, tobacco; wheat growers, wheat; and so on. Grain
producers may be completely at odds with poultrymen in
trying to keep grain prices up, while the poultrymen try to
bring them down. Yet each wishes to keep right on producing grain and raising chickens and looks to the government
to underwrite profits when surpluses or other manifestations
of the law of supply and demand threaten to depress them.

In these respects, farmers are no different from manufacturers, businessmen, labor union members, or any other of
the multifarious special interest groups that seek their fortunes in Washington. Economic representation has long since
established itself as an extra-constitutional feature of our government, and in a system of economic representation the producers of agricultural commodities have just as much right
to represent their interests as the producers of automobiles or
labor. The farmers have enjoyed two advantages however:
they have been overrepresented in Congress, and they have
had an unusual amount of public moral support. It is a well-
known fact that geographical representation as exemplified
by the United States Senate and, to a lesser extent, by the
single-member districts of the House of Representatives,
gives a disproportionately higher share of representatives to
agriculture than to industry. The latter is concentrated in

fourteen or fifteen states and, within those and the other states in which it appears, in and around cities. Farming, on the other hand, is spread all over the country. In all states Congressional districts are usually a decade or two behind the census in reflecting the actual distribution of population; and even in industrial states, owing to the wide distribution of the rural population, rural districts are consistently over-represented as compared with urban. So it is that more members of Congress are in close touch with agricultural than with industrial constituents.

This advantage is, if anything, exceeded by the moral prestige of farming, to which we have already alluded. The belief exists that farming is more than a business, that it is a way of life; and although farmers themselves seem to be more interested in earning a living, there can be no doubt that the concept of the way of life has greatly influenced policies conceived in the interest of the business. "Horn a farmer," says Mencken in one of his more violent *Prejudices*, "and you stand in contumacy to the platforms of all known parties, to the devout faith of all known statesmen, and to God." [16] We have a soft spot in our hearts for farming. Who talks of saving business or manufacturing as a way of life? Who does not lament an abandoned farm?

Since the overwhelming majority of American farmers are family farmers, these political advantages and the power and influence they convey might suffice to explain our concern for the institution they represent. But our interest in the family farm has deeper roots. One of the earliest, and by all odds the most famous, cultivators of these roots was Thomas Jefferson, often called the father of American agriculture as well as of American democracy. In Jefferson's view, the agrarian way of life and the democratic were synonymous, and both found their most perfect expression in the family

16. *Prejudices*, Fourth Series, "The Husbandman."

farm. The Jeffersonian ideal is a hardy perennial. In 1937, when President Roosevelt received the report of his Committee on Farm Tenancy, he declared it revealed "a grave problem of great magnitude and complexity."

The American dream of the family-size farm, owned by the family which operates it, has become more and more remote. The agricultural ladder, on which an energetic young man might ascend from hired man to tenant to independent owner, is no longer serving its purpose. . . . The agricultural ladder . . . has become a treadmill. . . . When fully half the total farm population of the United States no longer can feel secure, when millions of our people have lost their roots in the soil, action to provide security is imperative, and will be generally approved.[17]

The President was echoing the opinions of his Committee, which laid down as a general aim "establishment of family-size farms," called for specific policies to overcome their economic disadvantages, and concluded its report with this homily:

Sturdy rural institutions beget self-reliance and independence of judgment. Sickly rural institutions beget dependency and incapacity to bear the responsibilities of citizenship. . . . Vigorous and sustained action is required for restoring the impaired resources on whose preservation continuance of the democratic process in this country to no small extent depends.[18]

The Jeffersonian ideal has been translated into policy. In 1940 a committee representing all federal agencies concerned with agriculture stated that policy as follows:

The U.S. Department of Agriculture believes that the welfare of agriculture and of the Nation will be promoted by an agricultural land tenure pattern characterized by efficient family-size owner-operated farms, and one of the continuing major objec-

17. President's Message to Congress, Feb. 16, 1937. *Farm Tenancy*, p. 25.
18. *Ibid.*, pp. 13, 20.

tives of the Department will be the establishment and maintenance of such farms as the predominating operating farm unit in the United States.[19]

By 1947, the ideal had attained even greater stature. Under the terms of the Employment Act of 1946, the President is obliged to submit to Congress each year an Economic Report which amounts to a statement, on the highest possible authority, of the comprehensive national interests and public economic policy of the United States. The first such Report summed up these objectives as "an expanding economy of maximum production, employment and purchasing power under a system of free enterprise," and "preserving the family-sized farm." [20]

Full employment and production was a straightforward economic proposition. Maximum employment and production under a system of free enterprise and family farming was an economic proposition with political strings attached, strings of democratic political theory. According to the experts, we could have full employment and production in agriculture with half our present farm population, perhaps less. Family farming is for many crops more costly of labor than large-scale commercial or collective farming. An enclosure movement and a guiding concept of maximum food production at minimum cost, like the British, would reduce the farm population to its irreducible minimum and place American agriculture on the most efficient possible basis as a productive and commercial enterprise. With all of our technological advantages, a collectivist movement like the Russian might achieve the same results. Why not go the way of the British or the Russians? Partly because most American farmers were

19. Ezekiel, Mordecai, "Schisms in Agricultural Policy," *Journal of Farm Economics*, 1942, Vol. XXIV, p. 471.
20. *The Economic Report of the President*, January 8, 1947, Washington, 1947, pp. 32, 35.

family farmers and, for all their protestations to the contrary, constituted one of the most powerful—many would say the most powerful—political groups in Washington; partly because American agrarian tradition was opposed to it; and partly, also, because basic principles of democratic political theory supported that agrarian tradition. For the full significance of these ideas and principles we must look beyond the logic of economics into the illogicalities of history and politics.

Let us begin at the beginning, with the tradition.

CHAPTER TWO

The Jeffersonian Ideal

THERE IS no name in American history so intimately associated with the twofold theme of agrarianism and democracy as that of Thomas Jefferson. On the two hundredth
anniversary of his birth, in 1943, the entire American agricultural community paid tribute to him "as a man of abiding passion for the sacred rights of the common people, and
as one who, throughout his entire career, remained pre-
eminently and above all a farmer"—this from the preamble
to a joint resolution of Congress establishing the National
Agricultural Jefferson Bicentenary Committee, representing
the Department of Agriculture, the land-grant colleges, the
national farm organizations, the agricultural press, scientific
and learned agricultural societies, and the federal Office of
Education.[1] Not as a digression, but as an integral part of
the war effort in which American democracy was then engaged, the Bicentenary Committee spread the agrarian and
the democratic fame of Jefferson throughout the nation; and
at Monticello, on the two hundred and first anniversary of
his birthday, Secretary of Agriculture Claude Wickard ac-
claimed Jefferson as "father of the idea of the family-sized
farm." [2]

Historians might question the merits of this accolade, but

1. Senate Joint Resolution No. 47, House Joint Res. No. 114. For
   text of resolution and activities of the Bicentenary Committee, see
   Agricultural History, 1945, Vol. XIX, pp. 167-185.
2. Wickard, Claude R., "Thomas Jefferson—Founder of American
   Agriculture" (Address delivered at Monticello, April 13, 1944,
   the 201st anniversary of Jefferson's birth.), *Agricultural History*,
   1945, Vol. XIX, p. 179.

they cannot deny the fact of it. To living Americans, Jefferson is the foremost exemplar of agrarian democracy. No one believed so implicitly as he in a causal connection between the occupation of farming and the political system of democracy, and no one, before or since his time, has given that belief a greater impetus among his countrymen. His writings take us as near to the origin of the agrarian tradition as any American's; and this fact, together with his labors for the republican government of his day that became the democratic government of ours, commends them to us as the most representative American expression of the tradition.[3]

Jefferson did not originate the tradition. He appropriated it. It was centuries old when he first took notice of it. From time immemorial, agriculture had been exalted above all other human occupations. The writings of Aristotle, Xenophon, and Hesiod reflect its prestige among the ancient Greeks, as do those of Cicero, Virgil, Horace, Pliny, Cato, Varro, and Columella, among the Romans. It was Socrates who, in the pages of Xenophon, contributed to the French Physiocrats of the eighteenth century the motto, "Husbandry is the mother and nurse of the other arts. For when husbandry flourishes, all the other arts are in good fettle, but whenever the land is compelled to lie waste, the other arts . . . well-nigh perish." [4] Medieval and Renaissance writers venerated agriculture, and with the poets and essayists of the eighteenth century the veneration developed into a cult. Cicero spoke for them all, and for the host of writers since their day that has carried on their tradition, when he declared that "of all the occupations by which gain is secured, none is

3. The substance of this chapter appeared originally as "The Agrarian Democracy of Thomas Jefferson," *American Political Science Review*, August, 1946, Vol. XL, No. 4, pp. 657-681.
4. *Oeconomicus*, Loeb Transl., p. 405; Beer, M., *An Inquiry into Physiocracy*, London, 1939, p. 64; Gray, Alexander, *The Development of Economic Doctrine*, London, 1931, p. 30.

better than agriculture, none more profitable, none more delightful, none more becoming to a freeman." [5]

Much of this writing, all of it, perhaps, was an idealization of the circumstances in which men had lived and labored throughout most of their history. For thousands of years agriculture had been their principal means of livelihood. Even today it employs two-thirds of the human race. Only for a brief moment in history and in a few places on earth have men known anything but an agrarian environment. Since agriculture was the basic economic enterprise, the traditional calling of mankind, it is not surprising to find it sanctioned by religion, by secular idealism, by whatever forms in which the human propensity for rationalization found expression. Almost all men were farmers, therefore to think well of man was to think well of farming. As Cato says of his ancestors, "when they were trying to praise a good man they called him a good farmer and a good tiller of the soil, and the one who received this compliment was considered to have received the highest praise." [6] Man's universal respect for the producers of food, his first necessity, and his love of nature, which has grown as his distance from it has increased, have added mystic and romantic elements to the agrarian theme. Cicero was an indifferent farmer, an intellectual who enjoyed his country estates but whose chief contributions to agriculture were literary and forensic. He has had a numerous following: farmers have never lacked friends among writers and politicians. A farm is still the best place for a politician

5. *De Officiis*, I, xlii, Loeb Transl., p. 155; Gray, *op. cit.*, Ch. I; Johnstone, Paul H., "In Praise of Husbandry" and "Turnips and Romanticism," *Agricultural History*, Vol. XI, pp. 80-95, Vol. XII, pp. 224-255. Also "The Rural Socrates," *Journal of the History of Ideas*, 1944, Vol. V, pp. 151-175; Heitland, W. E., *Agricola*, Cambridge, 1921, *passim*.
6. *Cato, the Censor, on Farming* (Brehaut Transl.), Preface, p. 1.

to be born. The annual list of best sellers invariably contains a votive offering to the country.

The moral ascendancy of agriculture reached its peak during the second half of the eighteenth century in England and France. In those years, which saw the beginning of the industrial revolution in England and culminated in political revolutions in America and France, farming and rural life, the practical fulfillment of the increasingly popular philosophy of nature, became a craze among the British and French. British royalty and aristocracy vied with one another in enclosing and exploiting great agricultural estates. The enclosure movement, whose social consequences Goldsmith deplored in *The Deserted Village*, had its enthusiastic spokes-man in the agricultural writer Arthur Young. The farming gentry eagerly read Young, founded agricultural societies, introduced technical improvements on their estates, and turned husbandry into big business. The extent of the fashion may be measured by the fact that King George III himself operated a model farm at Windsor, contributed to Young's *Annals of Agriculture*, carried Young's books about with him when he traveled, and did not conceal his pleasure in the nickname "Farmer George." [7] "Perhaps," Arthur Young wrote, "we might, without any great impropriety, call farm-ing the reigning taste of the present times." [8]

In France, meanwhile, François Quesnay and his disciples, Mirabeau, Mercier de la Rivière, Le Trosne, and Du Pont de Nemours, were propounding an economic system known as Physiocracy, from the law of nature upon which it was based. The Physiocrats taught that all human affairs were governed by a divinely ordained natural order, *l'ordre naturel*, in which agriculture was the only productive occupation, the

---

7. Lord Ernle, *English Farming Past and Present*, London, 1912, pp. 196, 207; Johnstone, "Turnips and Romanticism," p. 233.
8. *Rural Economy*, p. 173; Johnstone, "The Rural Socrates," p. 161.

only true source of wealth. It was therefore the duty of the government to remove all taxes upon the land and its cultivators except a single tax on its net product, that is, after the deduction of costs. Apart from this, the state should keep its hands off economic enterprise: *laissez faire, laissez passer.* Whatever favored agriculture favored the public welfare; whatever harmed it was by definition unnatural and immoral. There were mixed motives in this as in all doctrines. The Physiocrats were applying John Locke's philosophy of natural rights to economic life, partly in conscientious protest against the tax-ridden mercantilist economy of Colbert, partly in the interests of a rising class of well-to-do bourgeois landowners (of whom Quesnay himself was one), who bought large estates, affected the manners of the nobility, and wanted to make money out of farming. Whatever their motives, by claiming divine sanction for agriculture as the sole source of wealth and the touchstone of human welfare, they carried its economic and moral prestige to its historic peak.[9]

It was against this background that Jefferson and his colleagues composed their thoughts on agriculture and the agrarian way of life. George Washington ran a model farm like George III, corresponded with Arthur Young about its management, and avowed that agriculture was "amongst the most favourite amusements" of his life.[10] Jefferson's political

9. Cf. Beer, M., *An Inquiry into Physiocracy*, London, 1939; Weulersse, G., *Le Mouvement Physiocratique en France de 1756 à 1770*, Paris, 1931; Gide, C., and Rist, C., *A History of Economic Doctrines*, London, 1932, Ch. I; Haney, L. H., *History of Economic Thought*, New York, 1924, Ch. IX; Ware, N. J., "The Physiocrats," *American Economic Review*, 1931, Vol. XXI, pp. 607-619.

10. Washington to Young, August 6, 1786. Knight, F., ed., *Letters on Agriculture from His Excellency George Washington, President of the United States to Arthur Young, Esq., F.R.S., and Sir John Sinclair, Bart., M.P.*, Washington, 1847, p. 16.

disciple and heir, James Madison, was one of the founders and early presidents of the Albermarle Agricultural Society of Virginia.[11] John Taylor, a fellow-planter from Caroline County, Virginia, has been called "the philosopher and statesman of agrarianism."[12] Jefferson was born to farming, as

11. Johnstone, Paul H., "Old Ideals versus New Ideas in Farming," in *Farmers in a Changing World*, U.S. Dept. of Agr. Yearbook, 1940, p. 114.

12. Beard, Charles A., *Economic Origins of Jeffersonian Democracy*, New York, 1927, p. 322. Taylor has also been called "the philosopher of Jeffersonian democracy"—Wright, B. F., Jr., "The Philosopher of Jeffersonian Democracy," *American Political Science Review*, 1928, Vol. XXII, pp. 870-892. But see Craven, A. O., "John Taylor and Southern Agriculture," *Journal of Southern History*, 1938, Vol. IV, pp. 137-147; Drell, Bernard, "John Taylor of Caroline and the Preservation of an Old Social Order," *Virginia Magazine of History and Biography*, 1938, Vol. XLVI, pp. 285-298; Mudge, E. T., *The Social Philosophy of John Taylor of Caroline*, New York, 1939, esp. pp. 5-6; Dauer, M. J., and Hammond, H., "John Taylor: Democrat or Aristocrat?", *Journal of Politics*, 1944, Vol. VI, pp. 381-403. The findings of these authorities substantially qualify Taylor's theory of democracy as, indeed, does a reading of his two main works, *Arator* (1803) and *An Inquiry into the Principles and Policy of the United States* (1814). From these documents it seems clear that Taylor's main interest was vested in the planter society to which he belonged and the decline of whose economic fortunes he was trying to reverse (a) by an intelligent and farsighted program of soil conservation, as set forth in *Arator*, and (b) by political actions and doctrines designed to check the advance of nationalism, commerce, and industry and adding up to a dialectic of states' rights. Although Jefferson acknowledged his indebtedness to Taylor, with whom he said he "rarely, if ever, differed in any political principle of importance" (Jefferson to Thomas Ritchie, December 25, 1820, *Works*, Vol. XII, p. 176; cf. same to Samuel Smith, April 12, 1821, *ibid.*, p. 203), to read them both, side by side, is to sense the fundamental difference between them. While Jefferson's writings on democracy and agrarianism are brief and fragmentary and Taylor's voluminous and systematic, Taylor's localism, both in time and place, and his intense partisanship make it impossible to accept him unreservedly as the philosopher of Jeffersonian democracy. An ardent agrarian he certainly was, going Jefferson one better in

were most of his countrymen. He loved the land, trying again and again to escape to it from "the hated occupations of politics." His years at Monticello were unquestionably his happiest. "I return to farming with an ardor which I scarcely knew in my youth," he wrote Adams in 1794,[13] and in later years:

I have often thought that if heaven had given me choice of my position and calling, it should have been on a rich spot of earth, well watered, and near a good market for the productions of the garden. No occupation is so delightful to me as the culture of the earth. . . .[14]

These were no idle sentiments. As his correspondence and notebooks show, his interest in farming was sincere and consistent throughout his life. They also reveal him as an experimental agriculturist of distinction. His observations and adaptations of European crops, livestock, and methods of farming put him in the vanguard of his contemporaries. He introduced the threshing machine in America and was one of the first importers of Merino sheep from Spain. His improved mold-board plow won him international awards. The

every claim of economic supremacy and moral perfection for agriculture. Likewise, as H. H. Simms (*Life of John Taylor*, Richmond, Va., 1932), Dauer and Hammond (*op. cit.*), and Arthur Schlesinger (*The Age of Jackson*, Boston, 1945) have depicted him, he was a last-ditch opponent of Federalism, more uncompromising than Jefferson himself. Yet he worked and thought primarily for a particular class, at a particular time, in a particular context of party politics, and these facts, together with his incredibly diffuse style, have limited his fame, while Jefferson's, resting on national achievement and universal principles, survives. The most authentic "philosopher of Jeffersonian democracy" is Jefferson, not Taylor.

13. *Works*, Vol. VIII, pp. 144-145. All references to Federal Edition, N. Y., 1904, unless otherwise indicated.
14. To Charles Willson Peale, August 20, 1811. *Writings*, Library Edition (Lipscomb and Bergh, eds.), Vol. XIII, pp. 78-80.

agricultural societies he founded and encouraged and his recommended inclusion of scientific agriculture in the curriculum of the University of Virginia foreshadowed our whole national system of agricultural education. Instead of patenting his innovations and improvements, moreover, he gave them freely to the public, and instead of profiting from them he ended his years in virtual bankruptcy. This he attributed to the "disgusting dish of politics" which had lured him from his chosen vocation and cost him proficiency in it.[15]

His political concern for agriculture was equally obvious. He had espoused the cause of the common man. At that time in our history, the common man was a farmer. Ninety per cent of all Americans, common or uncommon, were farmers. To champion the people, therefore, was to champion agriculture, a political theorem no politician could deny, however lofty or disinterested his purposes. The character of these people and their geographical surroundings might have determined their economic life without benefit of political theory. Lack of capital and a wilderness that yielded only to hard, slow manual labor made small-scale family farming the rule long before Jefferson became its advocate. The tobacco, rice, and cotton plantations of his southern compatriots were exceptions to the rule. It would be possible to ascribe his solicitude for small landholders to an astute rationalization of things as they were among his largest and most sympathetic political constituency.

But Jefferson was more than a farmer and a politician. He was a serious student of philosophy. The diligence with which he applied himself to his philosophical studies, to a search

15. Miller, August C., Jr., "Jefferson as an Agriculturist," *Agricultural History*, 1942, Vol. XVI, pp. 65-78; Wilson, M. L., "Thomas Jefferson—Farmer," American Philosophical Society *Proceedings*, 1943, Vol. LXXXVII, pp. 216-222.

for moral guidance and for counsels of law and government, is collateral for the sincerity of his political and economic ideas. We know from his letters and commonplace books the time and thought he devoted to the Greek and Latin classics, to Locke, Bolingbroke, Hume, Montesquieu, Adam Smith, Destutt de Tracy, and many another English and French writer represented on the shelves of his library.[16] We know from the Declaration of Independence, his principal state paper, the degree to which he had steeped himself in the natural rights philosophy of John Locke. During his residence in Paris (1784-1789), he made the acquaintance of the Physiocrat, Du Pont de Nemours, and the economist, Destutt de Tracy.

Du Pont, who took up residence in America, and whose son founded the "gunpowder manufactory" that was eventually to gain un-Physiocratic fame as the eighth largest industrial corporation in the United States,[17] became one of Jefferson's closest intellectual friends. Their correspondence over a period of seventeen years (1800-1817) weighed and appraised not only the principles of Physiocracy but most of the leading ideas of government and political economy current at the time. Jefferson's admiration for Destutt de Tracy was extravagant. He translated and edited De Tracy's *Commentary and Review of Montesquieu's Spirit of Laws* and his

16. For Jefferson's philosophical and literary sources, see especially Koch, Adrienne, *The Philosophy of Thomas Jefferson*, New York, 1943; Becker, Carl, *The Declaration of Independence*, New York, 1922; Chinard, G., ed., *The Commonplace Book of Thomas Jefferson*, Baltimore, 1926, *The Literary Bible of Thomas Jefferson*, Baltimore, 1928, and *The Correspondence of Thomas Jefferson and Du Pont de Nemours*, Baltimore, 1931; Chinard, G. (author), *Thomas Jefferson: The Apostle of Americanism*, Boston, 1929.

17. Moody's *Manual of Investments, Industrial Securities, 1945*, listed it as the eighth largest in financial assets in 1944.

Treatise on Political Economy, which he considered the leading works in "civil government" and political economy.[18]
He persuaded the president of his alma mater, William and
Mary, to adopt the *Commentary* as a text and spoke so
enthusiastically about it to his friends that Du Pont, for one,
accused him of having written it.[19]

What is of interest to us in all this intellectual trafficking
is not the genealogy of Jefferson's ideas, at best a speculative
theme, but their substance, the elements of which they were
composed, the process of composition. His general views on
agriculture may require no more complicated explanation
than, as already suggested, that they were perfectly logical
deductions from his own tastes and environment. Undoubt-
edly he found moral support for them in his reading, especially in the classics. But the character of the views, their
obviousness, generality, and fundamental simplicity, discour-
ages a search for more specific doctrinal influences. The
Physiocratic influence that is sometimes inferred in this connection has been discounted not only by historical scholars [20]
but by Jefferson himself. The inference derived largely from
their common emphasis of agriculture, the similarity of the
moral philosophy which both drew independently of each
other from Locke, and from Jefferson's friendship with Du
Pont. But Jefferson's homespun agrarianism stopped far short
of the elaborate "arithmetical formularies," as Adam Smith

18. Jefferson to Milligan, October 25, 1818, in Destutt de Tracy,
    A Treatise on Political Economy, Georgetown, 1817, foreword.
19. Chinard, *Correspondence of Jefferson and Du Pont*, p. 179; Koch,
    op. cit., Ch. VII.
20. The fullest discussion and evidence on this point are to be found
    in Chinard, *Correspondence of Jefferson and Du Pont*, Introduc-
    tion and *passim*. See also, Malone, Dumas, *Dictionary of American
    Biography*, Vol. X, p. 23; Hofstadter, R., "Parrington and the
    Jeffersonian Tradition," *Journal of the History of Ideas*, 1941,
    Vol. II, pp. 391-400.

called them,[21] by which Quesnay proved agriculture the sole source of wealth and a single tax upon its net product the best source of public revenue. As Chinard has pointed out,[22] Jefferson was never an economist in the formal sense of the word. There is no trace of Physiocratic or any other systematic economic analysis in any of his writings. He did not make Du Pont's acquaintance until some time during his tour of duty in Paris (1784-1789), nearly a decade after he had formulated and published his political philosophy, and at least two years after he had done the same with his views on agriculture. The latter he had set forth in his *Notes on Virginia,* which he had written in 1781 and revised in the winter of 1782-83. His exposure to the revolutionary intellectual ferment of Paris, far from revising his political opinions, strengthened them.

When he did enter into a specific discussion of Physiocratic economic policies in his correspondence with Du Pont, he exhibited a sturdy pragmatism and a practical sense of proportions which included commerce and industry, and to which, in the end, he partially converted Du Pont. Finally, in the "prospectus" to his edition of De Tracy's *Political Economy,* he stated his preference for Adam Smith, J. B. Say, and De Tracy, and disposed of Physiocracy thus:

Political Economy, in modern times, assumed the form of a regular science, first in the hands of the political sect in France, called the Economists. They made it a branch only of a comprehensive system, on the natural order of Societies. Quesnia [sic] first, Gournay, Le Trosne, Turgot, & Du Pont de Nemours, the enlightened, philanthropic, and venerable citizen now of the United States, led the way in these developments, and gave to our enquiries the direction they have since observed. Many sound and valuable principles, established by them, have received the sanction of gen-

21. *Wealth of Nations,* Modern Library, E. Cannan, ed., New York, 1937, p. 637.
22. *Thomas Jefferson,* p. 328.

eral approbation. Some, as in the infancy of a science, might be expected, have been brought into question, and have furnished occasion for much discussion; their opinions on production, and on the proper subjects of taxation, have been particularly controverted and whatever may be the merit of their principles of taxation, it is not wonderful that they have not prevailed, not on the questioned score of correctness, but because not acceptable to the people, whose will must be the supreme law. Taxation is, in fact, the most difficult function of government, and that against which, their citizens are most apt to be refractory. The general aim is, therefore, to adopt the mode most consonant with the circumstances and sentiments of the country.[23]

One fundamental difference between Jefferson and the Physiocrats brings out his own views on agriculture in sharp relief. The Physiocrats stood for large-scale farming and great estates, in conscious emulation of Arthur Young and the British aristocracy. They represented a group of prosperous magistrates and bureaucrats then rising in French society, seeking (and gaining) titles, and determined, like the British, to make their newly acquired estates pay. Quesnay, Mercier de la Rivière, and Du Pont himself were all men of this type. They believed in scientific estate farming, which they called *la grande culture;* and their single tax, which ensured the owner a comfortable margin of profit, was conceived in its interest.[24] The welfare of the peasants to them was of minor consideration, save in so far as all would gain from a simplification of the prevailing tax system. They favored, in other words, the interests of new and prosperous recruits to the landed aristocracy and proposed detailed methods of furthering those interests.

Jefferson from the outset directed his thoughts to small frontier farmers and never, even in their interest, conceived of economic measures so complex in detail or specific in pur-

23. De Tracy, *A Treatise on Political Economy*, p. iii.
24. Cf. authorities on Physiocracy cited above, esp. Ware.

pose as those of the Physiocrats. Agriculture, to him, was not primarily a source of wealth but of human virtues and traits most congenial to popular self-government. It had a sociological rather than an economic value. This is the dominant note in all his writings on the subject. In Europe, he says in his *Notes on Virginia*, manufacturing was being promoted to support the surplus population that could not gain access to the land.

But we have an immensity of land courting the industry of the husbandman. Is it best then that all our citizens should be employed in its improvement, or that one half should be called off from that to exercise manufactures and handicraft arts for the other? Those who labour in the earth are the chosen people of God, if ever He had a chosen people, whose breasts He has made His peculiar deposit for substantial and genuine virtue. It is the focus in which He keeps alive that sacred fire, which otherwise might escape from the face of the earth. Corruption of morals in the mass of cultivators is a phenomenon of which no age nor nation has furnished an example. It is the mark set on those, who, not looking up to heaven, to their own soil and industry, as does the husbandman, for their subsistence, depend for it on casualties and caprice of customers. Dependence begets subservience and venality, suffocates the germ of virtue, and prepares fit tools for the designs of ambition. This, the natural progress and consequence of the arts, has sometimes perhaps been retarded by accidental circumstances; but, generally speaking the proportion which the aggregate of the other classes of citizens bears in any state to that of its husbandmen, is the proportion of its unsound to its healthy parts, and is a good enough barometer whereby to measure its degree of corruption. While we have land to labour then, let us never wish to see our citizens occupied at a workbench, or twirling a distaff. Carpenters, masons, smiths, are wanting in husbandry; but, for the general operations of manufacture, let our workshops remain in Europe. It is better to carry provisions and materials to workmen there, than bring them to the provisions and materials, and with them their manners and principles. The loss by the transportation of commodities across the Atlantic will be made up in happiness and permanence of government. The mobs of great cities add just so much to the support of pure government, as sores do to the strength of the human body. It is the manners and spirit of a people which preserve a republic in vigor. A degeneracy in these is a canker which soon eats to the heart of its laws and constitution.[25]

This is a recurrent theme: "Cultivators of the earth are the most valuable citizens. They are the most vigorous, the most independent, the most virtuous, and they are tied to their country, and wedded to its liberty and interests by the most lasting bonds. . . . I consider the class of artificers as the panders of vice, and the instruments by which the liberties of a country are generally overturned." [26] Again: "I think our governments will remain virtuous for many centuries; as long as they are chiefly agricultural; and this will be as long as there shall be vacant lands in any part of America. When they get piled up upon one another in large cities, as in Europe, they will become corrupt as in Europe." [27] Jefferson came almost as near to claiming a monopoly of good morals for farmers as the Physiocrats did of the sources of material wealth.

He never changed these views, though he never permitted them or any other theoretical consideration to obscure his sense of the practical.[28] He had bitterly opposed Hamilton in the creation of a national bank (1790), having gone so far as to call the funding of the public debt an iniquitous and unconstitutional levy on farmers for the benefit of "stock-jobbers." Yet, when he became President, he maintained Ham-

25. *Works*, Vol. IV, pp. 85-86.
26. To John Jay, August 23, 1785. *Writings*, Vol. IV, pp. 449-450.
27. To James Madison, December 20, 1787. *Writings*, Vol. V, p. 374.
28. Cf. Dorfman, J., "The Economic Philosophy of Thomas Jefferson," *Political Science Quarterly*, 1940, Vol. LV, pp. 98-121, and *The Economic Mind in American Civilization*, New York, 1946, Vol. I, pp. 433-447. In his later work Mr. Dorfman calls Jefferson a "Commercial-Agrarian" and emphasizes Jefferson's practical interest in the commercial development of the United States.

ilton's policies. He had inherited the "half lettered ideas of Hamilton," he explained to Du Pont, but they were law and he was bound to defend them. "We can pay off his debt in 15 years but we can never get rid of his financial system. It mortifies me to be strengthened by principles which I deem radically vicious, but this vice is entailed on us by a just error." Then follows a sentence that provides the key to his whole character: "What is practicable must often countrol what is pure theory, and the habits of the governed determine in a great degree what is practicable." [29] He displays here that pragmatic empiricism which has governed Anglo-American political thought and action through history, confounding European critics in our time as it perplexed Du Pont in his. The logical Frenchman wanted things planned, ordered, consistent, directed from the top down, having no more faith than Hamilton in the capacity of the common people to know their own best interests. Jefferson's faith in the people was complete. He considered it "a duty in those entrusted with the administration of their affairs, to conform themselves to the decided choice of their constituents." [30] Toward the end of their long correspondence he admonished Du Pont: "We both consider the people as our children, and love them with parental affection. But you love them as infants whom you are afraid to trust without nurses, and I as adults, whom I freely leave to self government." [31]

True to this basic philosophy, which not infrequently drew charges of hypocrisy from his enemies, when the people began to manifest an interest in commerce and industry, Jefferson

29. Jefferson to Du Pont, January 18, 1802. Chinard, *Correspondence*, p. 37.
30. Jefferson to John Jay, August 23, 1785. *Works*, Vol. IV, p. 450.
31. Jefferson to Du Pont, April 24, 1816. Chinard, *Correspondence*, p. 258.

went along with them. This is how he answered a direct query on the point in 1785:

You ask what I think on the expediency of encouraging our States to be commercial? Were I to indulge my own theory, I should wish them to practice neither commerce nor navigation, but to stand, with respect to Europe, precisely on the footing of China. We should thus avoid wars, and all our citizens would be husbandmen. Whenever, indeed, our numbers should so increase as that our produce would overstock the markets of those nations who should come to seek it, the farmers must either employ the surplus of their time in manufactures, or the surplus of our hands must be employed in manufactures or in navigation. But that day would, I think, be distant, and we should long keep our workmen in Europe, while Europe should be drawing rough materials, and even subsistence from America. But this is theory only, and a theory which the servants of America are not at liberty to follow.[32]

Again the practical qualifications, the acceptance of what was in place of what ought to be. A quarter century later, he had moved so far with the times as to prescribe an "equilibrium of agriculture, manufactures, and commerce":

Manufactures, sufficient for our own consumption, of what we raise the raw material (and no more). Commerce sufficient to carry the surplus produce of agriculture, beyond our own consumption, to a market for exchanging it for articles we cannot raise (and no more). These are the true limits of manufactures and commerce. . . . These three important branches of human industry will then grow together, and be really handmaids to each other.[33]

Finally, in 1816, this thoroughgoing discussion of the matter:

You tell me I am quoted by those who wish to continue our dependence on England for manufactures. There was a time when

32. Jefferson to Count Gysbert-Charles van Hogendorp, October 13, 1785. *Works*, Vol. IV, pp. 466-470.
33. Jefferson to James Jay, April 7, 1809. *Writings*, Library ed. (Lipscomb and Bergh), Vol. XII, pp. 270-271.

I might have been so quoted with more candor, but within the thirty years which have since elapsed, how are circumstances changed! We were then in peace. Our independent place among the nations was acknowledged. A commerce which offered the raw material in exchange for the same material after receiving the last touch of industry, was worthy of welcome to all nations. It was expected that those especially to whom manufacturing industry was important, would cherish the friendship of such customers by every favor, by every inducement, and particularly cultivate their peace by every act of justice and friendship. Under this prospect the question seemed legitimate, whether, with such an immensity of unimproved land, courting the hand of husbandry, the industry of agriculture, or that of manufactures, would add most to the national wealth? And the doubt was entertained on this consideration chiefly, that to the labor of the husbandman a vast addition is made by the spontaneous energies of the earth on which it is employed: for one grain of wheat committed to the earth, she renders twenty, thirty, and even fifty fold, whereas to the labor of the manufacturer nothing is added. Pounds of flax, in his hands, yield, on the contrary, but pennyweights of lace. This exchange, too, laborious as it might seem, what a field did it promise for the occupations of the ocean; what a nursery for that class of citizens who were to exercise and maintain our equal rights on that element? This was the state of things in 1785, when the "Notes on Virginia" were first printed; when, the ocean being open to all nations, and their common right in it acknowledged and exercised under regulations sanctioned by the assent and usage of all, it was thought that the doubt might claim some consideration. But who in 1785 could foresee the rapid depravity which was to render the close of that century the disgrace of the history of man? Who could have imagined that the two most distinguished in the rank of nations, for science and civilization, would have suddenly descended from that honorable eminence, and setting at defiance all those moral laws established by the Author of nature between nation and nation, as between man and man, would cover earth and sea with robberies and piracies, merely because strong enough to do it with temporal impunity; and that under this disbandment of nations from social order, we should have been despoiled of a thousand ships, and have thousands of our citizens reduced to Algerine slavery. Yet all this has taken place. . . . Compare this state of things with that of '85, and say whether an opinion founded in the circumstances of that day can be fairly applied to those of the present. We have experienced what we did not then believe, that there exists both profligacy and power enough to exclude us from the field of interchange with other nations: that to be independent for the comforts of life we must fabricate them ourselves. We must now place the manufacturer by the side of the agriculturist. The former question is suppressed, or rather assumes a new form. Shall we make our own comforts, or go without them, at the will of a foreign nation? He, therefore, who is now against domestic manufacture, must be for reducing us either to dependence on that foreign nation, or to be clothed in skins, and to live like wild beasts in dens and caverns. I am not one of these; experience has taught me that manufactures are now as necessary to our independence as to our comfort. . . .[34]

Several features of Jefferson's conversion are of interest. In the first place, it was incomplete. The farthest he would go was to approve a balanced, self-sufficient economy in which he expected agriculture to occupy the most important position. Secondly, it was reluctant: he attributed it to the "depravity" of the times. Thirdly, it was decided not on the merits of the question but by international politics and war. The Napoleonic Wars were not the first in which American domestic issues had been confused by the whims and ambitions of foreign powers, nor would they be the last. The dominant role they played in the conversion of Jefferson, if we may call it such, shows the extent to which the conversion was one of expediency rather than of principle. The world war in which we became a belligerent in 1812 forced him to forego as statesman and patriot views which, as farmer and philosopher, he never formally renounced. To the end of his days, agriculture remained the occupation nearest his heart, his ideal of a good society: a society of farmers.

34. Jefferson to Benjamin Austin, January 9, 1816. *Works*, Vol. XI, pp. 502-505.

We should say, as he did, a society of small farmers, for as we shall see, he considered these "the most precious part of a state." [35] The political freedom of the individual was his *summum bonum,* and the political value that Jefferson expected agriculture to yield was exactly that, a value best produced on a small farm. For it was pre-eminently on a small farm that those qualities of independence and self-reliance, of "looking up to heaven, to their own soil and industry," that were most readily convertible into enlightened self-government were most thoroughly developed in farmers. Political independence rested upon social equality and economic security, of which a small farm was the surest foundation. The tiller of another man's fields could never feel the sense of economic security nor the pride of possession of the independent farmer, still less could those dependent upon "casualties and caprice of customers . . . or twirling a distaff." Democracy meant self-government. Who would govern himself must own his soul. To own his soul he must own property, the means of economic security. Everyone in America could own land. Thus everyone, "by his property, or by his satisfactory situation, is interested in the support of law and order. And such men may safely and advantageously reserve to themselves a wholesome control over their public affairs. . . ." [36] The typical form of private property was land, and the typical use for land was farming. Thus we find in Jefferson's conception of the property right another link between his agrarianism and his democracy.

A search for the intellectual basis of this conception again leads back to Locke. "The earth is given as a common stock for man to labour and live on," Jefferson wrote from Paris in 1785. The "right to labour the earth" was "funda-

---

35. Cf. below, p. 45, note 57.
36. Jefferson to Adams, October 28, 1813, *Works,* Vol. XI, p. 348.

mental." [37] And in 1816, in a detailed summary of his political creed, he stated the belief "that a right of property is founded in our natural wants, in the means with which we were endowed to satisfy these wants, and the right to what we acquire by those means without violating the similar rights of other sensible beings." [38] A century and a quarter earlier, Locke had written:

God, who hath given the world to men in common, hath also given them reason to make use of it to the best advantage of life and convenience. The earth and all that is therein is given to men for the support and comfort of their being. And though all the fruits it naturally produces, and beasts it feeds, belong to mankind in common, as they are produced by the spontaneous hand of Nature, and nobody has originally a private dominion exclusive of the rest of mankind in any of them, as they are thus in their natural state, yet being given for the use of men, there must of necessity be a means to appropriate them some way or other before they can be of any use, or at all beneficial, to any particular men. [39]

Even the phrasing sounds like Jefferson's, and both echo the psalm Locke quotes as his authority: "The heaven, even the heavens, are the Lord's: but the earth hath he given to the children of men." [40]

Whether consciously or indirectly and unconsciously borrowed from Locke, Jefferson's theory of property was essentially Locke's. What was Locke's in essence had evolved out of pre-Christian custom, Roman law, and medieval doctrine to find philosophical definition at Locke's hands and to be transmitted by him to most political philosophers of the

37. Cf. below, p. 45, note 57.
38. Jefferson to Du Pont, April 24, 1816. Chinard, *Correspondence*, p. 258.
39. Locke, *Two Treatises of Civil Government*, Book II, Ch. V, par. 25.
40. Psalm 115, verse 16.

eighteenth, and many of the nineteenth, century. By the time
Locke's ideas on property had reached Jefferson, many tribu-
taries had flowed into the stream, broad as it was even in
Locke's day. The texts Jefferson studied at William and
Mary, the authorities he consulted as a law student, the more
specific writings, such as Kames' *Historical Law Tracts*, that
he extracted in his commonplace book, all reflected the general sanction civilized society had long since placed upon the
institution of private property.

The colonists had brought this sanction with them to
America. The Protestant churches, to which most of them belonged, had improved upon it with the doctrine of the calling, according to which material possessions were a proof of
virtue and a sign of heavenly grace.[41] Taxation without representation, the *cause célèbre* of the Revolution, had made
every American acutely conscious of the property right and
its relation to government. The first resolution of the Declaration and Resolves of the First Continental Congress, October 14, 1774, proclaimed the right "to life, liberty and
property." Jefferson's own draft of the Declaration on Taking up Arms, July 6, 1775, declared: "The political institutions of America, its various soils and climates opened a certain resource to the unfortunate and to the enterprising of
every country and ensured to them the acquisition and free
possession of property." [42] The first resolution of the famous
Virginia Bill of Rights, written by George Mason, adopted
June 12, 1776, and honored by imitation in both America and
France read:

41. Cf. Tawney, R. H., *Religion and the Rise of Capitalism*, New
York, 1926; Weber, Max, *The Protestant Ethic and the Spirit of
Capitalism*, London, 1930; Griswold, A. Whitney, "Three Puri-
tans on Prosperity," *New England Quarterly*, 1934, Vol. VII,
pp. 475-493.
42. *Works*, Vol. II, p. 113.

That all men are by nature equally free and independent, and have certain inherent rights, of which, when they enter into a state of society, they cannot by any compact deprive or divest their posterity; namely, the enjoyment of life and liberty, with the means of acquiring and possessing property, and pursuing and obtaining happiness and safety.[43]

Property, in this context, was the means of freedom, not the end—as it later became. The right to private property was taken for granted, and the duty of the government to protect it assumed, by Jefferson when he sat down to compose the Declaration of Independence, and that document is anything if not representative of the times. When some of his contemporaries criticized it as "a commonplace compilation, its sentiments hacknied in Congress for two years before" and "as copied from Locke's treatise on Government," [44] Jefferson explained that he was not trying to invent new principles or ideas "but to place before mankind the common sense of the subject, in terms so plain and firm as to command their respect"; that the Declaration was intended as "an expression of the American mind" based on "the harmonizing sentiments of the day." [45]

In England, Locke's ideas on property were construed in the interests of the rich as well as the poor, whereas to Jefferson they provided the moral basis for a pattern of small landowners. The substance of these ideas was that the right to private property existed in the state of nature that preceded formal government. Although the earth and its fruits were given to mankind in common, a man's person and his labor were his and his alone. "Whatsoever, then, he removes

43. Commager, H. S., ed., *Documents of American History*, N. Y., 1946, No. 67.
44. Jefferson to James Madison, August 30, 1823. *Works*, Vol. XII, pp. 306-309.
45. Jefferson to Henry Lee, May 8, 1825. *Works*, Vol. XII, pp. 408-409.

out of the state that Nature hath provided and left it in, he hath mixed his labour with it, and joined to it something that is his own, and thereby makes it his property." [46] By picking up fruit or tilling a field or filling his pitcher at a fountain, a man appropriated exclusively to himself what was given by nature to all men equally and in common, with two important qualifications: there must be "enough, and as good left in common for others," [47] and no one must take more than he can use. Upon this second qualification Locke placed special emphasis:

It will, perhaps, be objected to this, that if gathering the acorns or other fruits of the earth, etc., makes a right to them, then any one may engross as much as he will. To which answer, Not so. The same law of Nature that does by this means give us property, does also bound that property too. "God has given us all things richly." Is the voice of reason confirmed by inspiration? But how far has He given it us—"to enjoy"? As much as any one can make use of to any advantage of life before it spoils, so much he may by his labour fix a property in. Whatever is beyond this is more than his share, and belongs to others. [48]

Applied to land, which Locke called "the chief matter of property," this meant "as much land as a man tills, plants, improves, cultivates, and can use the product of." [49] Thus defined and qualified, the natural right to private property must be recognized and protected by government as a basic condition of the social order. [50]

46. Locke, *Two Treatises of Civil Government*, Book II, Ch. V, par. 26.
47. *Idem.*
48. *Ibid.*, par. 30.
49. *Ibid.*, par. 31.
50. Locke, *Of Civil Government*, Book II, Ch. V. Cf. Larkin, Paschal, *Property in the 18th Century with Special Reference to England and Locke*, Dublin, 1930, esp. Ch. III; Lamprecht, S. P., *The Moral and Political Philosophy of John Locke*, New York, 1918, pp. 123-125; Aaron, R. I., *John Locke*, London, 1937, pp. 279-280.

The qualifications are important. Both Locke and Jefferson believed they would be automatically enforced by the great "immensity of land" behind the American frontier. Where they failed, according to Locke, was in those parts of the world where the increase of population "with the use of money" made land scarce and caused its distribution to be regulated "by compact and agreement." Where there was plenty of land and a minimum of commerce, "there men will not be apt to enlarge their possessions of land, were it never so rich, never so free for them to take."

For I ask, what would a man value ten thousand or an hundred thousand acres of excellent land, ready cultivated and well stocked, too, with cattle, in the middle of the inland parts of America, where he had no hopes of commerce with other parts of the world, to draw money to him by the sale of the product? It would not be worth the enclosing, and we should see him give up again to the wild common of Nature whatever was more than would supply the conveniences of life, to be had there for him and his family. Thus, in the beginning, all the world was America . . .[51]

Was this not a suggestion to Jefferson by the foremost political philosopher of the age, of a fall from grace and a hope of redemption in a rural democracy across the seas?

Here, surely, was confirmation, if not inspiration, for his ideal community of small landholders. If Locke was more interested in defending the right to private property than in promoting its equal division, to Jefferson both were important. Like Locke, he wished to make the strongest possible political case for the principle, as Locke put it, that "the supreme power cannot take from any man any part of his property without his own consent."[52] But the beneficiaries of the principle as Jefferson conceived it were small frontier farmers, not landed Parliamentarians as was the case with Locke.

51. Locke, *Of Civil Government*, Book II, pars. 45-49.
52. *Ibid.*, par. 138.

Locke's limitations on landowning came to the fore in Jefferson's thinking. There was a hint of them in the constitution he drew up for the state of Virginia in June, 1776, one title of which provided that every person of full age who neither owned nor had owned fifty acres of land should be entitled to an appropriation of fifty acres "in full and absolute dominion. And no other person shall be capable of taking an appropriation." [53]

There was more than a hint of them in the laws he drew up to abolish primogeniture and entail. So vital did he consider these that he obtained leave from Congress soon after the adoption of the Declaration of Independence to return to the Virginia legislature and see that they were carried out in his own state. He first brought in a bill doing away with entail, the means by which "a distinct set of families who, being privileged by law in the perpetuation of their wealth were thus formed into a Patrician order."

To annul this privilege, and instead of an aristocracy of wealth, of more harm and danger, than benefit, to society, to make an opening for the aristocracy of virtue and talent, which nature has wisely provided for the direction of the interests of society, and scattered with equal hand through all its conditions, was deemed essential to a well ordered republic. To effect it no violence was necessary, no deprivation of natural right, but rather an enlargement of it by a repeal of the law. For this would authorize the present holder to divide the property among his children equally, as his affections were divided; and would place them by natural generation on the level of their fellow citizens.[54]

Next he turned his attention to primogeniture:

As the Law of Descents, & the criminal law fell of course within my portion, I wished the commee [sic.] to settle the leading principles of these, as a guide for me in framing them. And with respect to the first, I proposed to abolish the law of primogeniture,

53. *Works*, Vol. II, p. 179.
54. *Works*, Vol. I, pp. 58-59.

and to make real estate descendible in parcenary to the next of kin, as personal property is by the statute of distribution. Mr. Pendleton wished to preserve the right of primogeniture, but seeing at once that that could not prevail, he proposed we should adopt the Hebrew principle, and give a double portion to the elder son. I observed that if the eldest son could eat twice as much, or do double work, it might be a natural evidence of his right to a double portion; but being on a par in his powers & wants, with his brothers and sisters, he should be on a par also in the partition of the patrimony, and such was the decision of the other members.[55]

These bills he considered "as forming a system by which every fibre would be eradicated of ancient or future aristocracy; and a foundation laid for a government truly republican."

The repeal of the laws of entail would prevent the accumulation and perpetuation of wealth in select families, and preserve the soil of the country from being daily more and more absorbed in Mortmain. The abolition of primogeniture, and equal partition of inheritances removed the feudal and unnatural distinctions which made one member of every family rich, and all the rest poor, substituting equal partition, the best of all Agrarian laws.[56]

Jefferson was too shrewd a politician to believe that a perfectly equal division of the land was possible. It was another of those ideals that he tried to realize pragmatically, as practical politics and human nature would permit. Yet it was an ideal. In a letter he wrote from Fontainebleau to the president of William and Mary College in 1785, he reduced the whole subject to its simplest terms. He was inspired to write by a chance encounter with an old peasant woman who had guided him on a walk through the countryside and answered his questions about "the condition of the labouring poor."

55. *Ibid.*, pp. 68-69.
56. *Ibid.*, pp. 77-78.

When he had rewarded her for this service with twenty-four sous, she had burst into tears of gratitude.

This little *attendrissement*, with the solitude of my walk, led me into a train of reflections on that unequal division of property which occasions the numberless instances of wretchedness which I had observed in this country & is to be observed all over Europe. The property of this country is absolutely concentrated in a very few hands, having revenues of from half a million of guineas a year downwards. These employ the flower of the country as servants, some of them having as many as 200 domestics, not labouring. They employ also a great number of manufacturers, & tradesmen, & lastly the class of labouring husbandmen. But after all there comes the most numerous of all the classes, that is, the poor who cannot find work. I asked myself what could be the reason that so many should be permitted to beg who are willing to work, in a country where there is a very considerable proportion of uncultivated lands? These lands are undisturbed only for the sake of game. It should seem then that it must be because of the enormous wealth of the proprietors which places them above attention to the encrease of their revenues by permitting these lands to be laboured. I am conscious that an equal division of property is impracticable. But the consequences of this enormous inequality producing so much misery to the bulk of mankind, legislators cannot invent too many devices for subdividing property, only taking care to let their subdivisions go hand in hand with the natural affections of the human mind.

The descent of property of every kind therefore to all the children, or to all the brothers & sisters, or other relations in equal degree is a politic measure and a practicable one. Another means of silently lessening the inequality of property is to exempt all from taxation below a certain point, & to tax the higher portions of property in geometrical progression as they rise. Whenever there is in any country, uncultivated lands and unemployed poor, it is clear that the laws of property have been so far extended as to violate natural right. The earth is given as a common stock for man to labour & live on. If for the encouragement of industry we allow it to be appropriated, we must take care that other employment be provided to those excluded from the appropriation. If we do not the fundamental right to labour the earth returns to the unemployed. It is too soon yet in our country to say that every man who cannot find employment but who can find uncultivated land shall be at liberty to cultivate it, paying a moderate rent. But it is not too soon to provide by every possible means that as few as possible shall be without a little portion of land. The small land holders are the most precious part of a state.[57]

The ancient agrarian tradition; the personal love of the soil; the theory of natural rights bequeathed by Locke to all liberal politicians of the age; the cause of American independence which became the cause of popular government versus the government of kings; the existing circumstances of the American frontier; the horror of the industrial revolution, fed by imagination as much as by a fleeting impression of England; the conception of the earth as a common stock; the immensity of land with which America might redeem Europe's loss; the belief in individual freedom and in private property as its means; the fact that farm land was the most typical and useful form of private property—the philosophical insight and the political sagacity—what does it matter which came first? All were present in the conclusion that small landholders, i.e., family farmers, were "the most precious part of a state," the classic American statement of the political theory of the family farm.

Are they still the most precious part of the state? Were they ever? Jefferson's dream of a rural republic, isolated from European commercialism and industrialism and composed entirely of self-governing farmers, had begun to fade before it was full-blown. As the intransigent John Taylor lamented to Monroe in 1810, "There were a number of people who soon thought, and said to one another, that Mr. Jefferson did many good things, but neglected some better things; and who now view his policy as very like a compro-

57. Jefferson to Rev. James Madison, Oct. 28, 1785. *Works*, Vol. VIII, pp. 194-196.

mise with Mr. Hamilton's." [58] Although Taylor continued to prompt him with such sentiments as "the divine intelligence which selected an agricultural state as a paradise for its first favourites, has . . . prescribed the agricultural virtues as the means for the admission of their posterity into heaven," [59] and to sandbag the dikes with ponderous arguments, both he and Jefferson saw that the rising tide of commerce and industry could not be held in check. The unpent genie of industrialism was moving about the world and had visited America. By 1791, Hamilton could say with confidence, in his *Report on Manufactures,* "The expediency of encouraging manufactures in the United States, which was not long since deemed very questionable, appears at this time to be pretty generally admitted." [60] So it came to be, even by Thomas Jefferson. But his ideal of democracy as a community of family farms has lived on to inspire the modern lawmakers and color the thoughts of their constituents when they turn their minds to rural life.

58. Taylor to Monroe, October 26, 1810. Dauer, M. J., and Hammond, H., *John Taylor: Democrat or Aristocrat,* p. 397.
59. *Arator,* 6th ed. (1818), p. 189. This was the most widely read of all Taylor's works, running through seven editions from 1803 to 1840. Mudge, E. T., *The Social Philosophy of John Taylor,* New York, 1939, p. 152.
60. Hamilton, *Works* (Constitutional Edition), Vol. IV, p. 70.

CHAPTER THREE

The British Experience

I T WAS in England, toward the middle of the eighteenth century, that the forces which gave the Jeffersonian ideal its present-day meaning were set in motion. When, as Locke put it, "all the world was America," when the agrarian was everywhere the prevailing way of life, its followers were not so anxious for political preferment as when industry arose to challenge it. Nor was there, in those early times, any such clearly defined conception of democracy as Jefferson's, not to mention our own. The democratic terms in which the Greeks had praised agriculture differed from Jefferson's in important particulars: in their assumption of slavery, for instance. After the decline of the Greek city states, democracy lay dormant in the world until its modern reawakening, nearly two thousand years later. England saw not only the beginning of the industrial revolution but also the first glimmerings of modern democratic thought, that were to culminate in the American and French revolutions and the slow evolution of democracy in Great Britain.

Notwithstanding practical differences, particularly in the social sphere, that democracy has come to resemble our own so closely in fundamentals that we might logically expect a general truth relating to democracy to be demonstrable in the history of either country. What, then, of the Jeffersonian ideal in the experience of the British? Have they believed in the generic relationship of democracy and the family farm? An outstanding American agricultural historian has declared: "The agricultural history of the United States is more closely related to that of Great Britain than to that of any other country. Our colonial forefathers brought with them the rural customs and practices of the Mother Country, and we as a nation continued through the nineteenth century to look mainly to England for leadership and example in agricultural improvement." [1] Can the same be said of our agrarian political philosophy?

For England, as for every other country that has followed in her wake, the industrial revolution meant an abrupt and painful conversion from farming to manufacturing, and from rural to city life. It was abrupt in that—although its conclusion is not yet—it altered profoundly, in hardly more than a century, the economic and social practices of the past two thousand years. It was painful because accomplished at the cost of human suffering of such proportions as to inspire a literature of protest to which poets and novelists contributed no less fervidly than the author of *Das Kapital*. From remote origins in the preceding century, some of which were French as well as British, the industrial revolution gathered momentum and by 1760 developed into a predominant force in England's social life. With its onset began a rural exodus that has repeated itself, to a greater or lesser degree, in each succeeding country to which it has spread. While the total British population grew from 7,000,000 in 1751 to 27,000,000 in 1851 and 45,000,000 in 1931, the agricultural population decreased until it was the smallest, proportionately, of any country in the world. From an estimated 28 per cent of the *total* population in 1831 (roughly 4,600,000 out of 16,500,000), it sank to 5.6 per cent of the *working* population (or 1,194,000 out of 21,055,000) in 1931. Meanwhile the number of persons employed in manufacturing and mining had risen, by the same year, to 31 per cent of the work-

1. Edwards, Everett E., *Selected References on the History of English Agriculture*, Washington, 1935, p. iii.

ing population.[2] Thus did the home of our rural customs and agricultural techniques give itself over to industrialism.

The first and most obvious conclusion to be drawn from these statistics is that the British did not share Jefferson's fears of commerce and industry. The second is that they did not identify democracy with the agrarian way of life. This is implicit in the fact that the rise of democracy in Great Britain coincided with the decline of the British farm population to the smallest proportions in the world. It is explicit in the economic and social pattern of British agriculture.

A French economist has called Great Britain, in contrast to western Europe, "the classical land of large estates and extensive farms."[3] Approximately 450,000 holdings devoted to agriculture or quasi-agricultural purposes were counted in Great Britain in 1937, of which 21 per cent, comprising 67 per cent of the total agricultural land, were over 100 acres in size. This does not make Great Britain wholly a country of large farms; but neither is it a country of chopped-up parcels and small holdings.[4] By comparison with the 4,000,000 agricultural holdings in France, of which only 4 per cent, comprising 30 per cent of the land, are over 125 acres and

2. Figures compiled from *Tables of the Revenue, Population, Commerce, etc., of the United Kingdom, Part III, 1820 to 1833*, esp. pp. 434-439; *Statistical Abstract for the United Kingdom*, 1938; Clapham, J. H., *An Economic History of Modern Britain*, Cambridge, 1939, Vol. I, Ch. II, Vol. II, pp. 22 ff.; Carr-Saunders, A. M., and Jones, D. C., *A Survey of the Social Structure of England and Wales*, Oxford, 1937, Ch. IV. The final British population figure does not include the net loss to migration of nearly 11,000,000 from 1800 to 1931.

3. Mantoux, Paul, *The Industrial Revolution in the Eighteenth Century*, New York, 1935, p. 140.

4. Venn, J. A., *Foundations of Agricultural Economics*, Cambridge, 1933, pp. 109, 117, estimates the average size of all British farms over 1 acre at 64 acres, as compared with a German and French average of about 15 acres.

no fewer than 1,000,000 are under 2½ acres in size, the extent of large-scale farming in Britain is impressive. The French figures are typical of a nation that has cherished the small peasant farm, the British, of a nation that has not.[5] Moreover, it is estimated that about 150,000 of the total British holdings consisted of "odd parcels of land used for an infinite variety of non-agricultural purposes such as recreation grounds, paddocks, butchers' accommodation grazing, private gardens, brewers' yards, unoccupied derelict holdings," and the like;[6] 134,000 were small holdings, and 55,000 were over 150 acres in size. This left the total of bona fide family farms—those of from 50 to 150 acres—at not more than 110,000[7]—a small number had they been considered the pillars of democracy.

That they were not so considered, that the Jeffersonian ideal has had no such appeal in Great Britain as it has in the United States, is evident in nearly every step of Britain's progress through the industrial revolution. Two striking illustrations are the enclosure movement of the late eighteenth and early nineteenth centuries, and the repeal of the Corn Laws in 1846. The first completed the process, begun several centuries earlier, of consolidating the historic open fields and commons in compact holdings under individual ownership and management. The second committed the nation to free trade. Both contributed substantially to the decline of the

5. Comparative figures on British and French farms from Great Britain, Ministry of Agriculture and Fisheries, *Agricultural Statistics*, 1939, Vol. LXXIV, Part I; Astor and Rowntree, eds., *British Agriculture*, London, 1938, pp. 358-360; Menzies-Kitchin, A. W., *The Future of British Farming*, London, 1945, pp. 40-41; *Statistical Abstract for the United Kingdom*, 1938, pp. 293; Yates, P. Lamartine, *Food Production in Western Europe*, London, 1940, pp. 273-275.
6. Astor and Rowntree, *op. cit.*, p. 358.
7. *Ibid.*, pp. 358-359; Menzies-Kitchin, *op. cit.*, p. 40.

agricultural population and the reduction almost to the vanishing point of the independent farmer who owned and occupied his own land.

When the industrial revolution began, British farmers had made little or no advance on the agricultural practices of the thirteenth century.[8] Spurred on by the experiments and writings of Jethro Tull (1674-1740), Arthur Young (1741-1820), and others, however, the gentry took up farming as a business and precipitated an agrarian revolution that accompanied the industrial. Opinions differ as to the precise interrelationship of these two phenomena, but in the perspective of history they merge in a general trend of capitalism and commerce. The industrial revolution stimulated the agrarian in several ways: by creating in the rapidly increasing industrial population a new and apparently insatiable market for foodstuffs; by contributing to agriculture new organizational and mechanical techniques; and by providing employment for the surplus agricultural labor these created. On the other hand, the agrarian revolution made the industrial revolution possible by supplying the greatly increased quantities of food required by its workers.[9] Both were surrounded by an atmosphere of commercial enterprise and accelerated by the needs of national self-sufficiency growing out of the Napoleonic Wars.

It was in these circumstances that the British gentry set about enlarging and consolidating its already extensive holdings of agricultural land, and prosperous businessmen and farmers followed their example. The framework of land ownership and rural society within which they operated was of complex medieval design. There was no free land. All of

8. Lord Ernle, *English Farming, Past and Present*, London, 1936, pp. 194 ff.
9. Cf. Mantoux, *Industrial Rev.*, Ch. III; Ernle, *English Farming*, pp. 205-206.

it was owned, for the most part by great landlords who had inherited it and either cultivated it, used it as pasture, leased it to tenants, or held it in huge parks, wastes, or game preserves. A smaller portion of the land was owned and cultivated by a more numerous class of squires and small independent farmers or "freeholders." These were in turn outnumbered by an elaborately stratified society of copyholders, tenant farmers, cottagers, and day laborers, varying in status from that of a prosperous modern tenant farmer at the top to that of a share-cropper or hired laborer at the bottom. Whatever independence these less-favored rural classes enjoyed they owed to the possession or lease of a strip or two in the open fields surrounding their villages and rights to pasture their livestock on the village commons and cut wood or dig peat in the unenclosed wastes.

When the industrial revolution, and with it the last great enclosure movement, began, over half the agricultural land of Britain consisted of strip-cultivated open fields and fenceless wastes and commons. There had been a wave of enclosures in the fifteenth and sixteenth centuries to provide sheep pasturage for the suppliers of the new wool trade, and the process had been more or less continuous ever since. Though it caused great distress, it was of comparatively slight proportions; from 1455 to 1637 only about 744,000 acres, or 2.1 per cent of the total area of England, were enclosed. Approximately 300,000 acres more were enclosed from 1700 to 1760. All of this was as nothing compared to the movement which enclosed well over 6,000,000 acres, or 20 per cent of the total area of England, from 1761 to 1900, more than 5,000,000 acres of it from 1761 to 1845.[10] When it

10. Figures from Curtler, W. H. R., *The Enclosure and Redistribution of Our Land*, Oxford University Press, 1920, pp. 139 ff., 148. This account of the enclosure movement is based on Curtler; Ernle, *English Farming*; Clapham, *Econ. Hist. Mod. Brit.*; Man-

finally came to an end there was practically no agricultural land left to enclose, and what waste land there was had been made the object of protective legislation by an urbanized society repining for its rural past.

Whatever else may be said about it, the enclosure movement concentrated the agricultural land of Britain in few hands and large units, bearing in this respect a striking resemblance to the pattern of industrialization. That it increased the efficiency of British agriculture does not alter its social and political significance. It was anything but democratic in character. Both the Tudor and eighteenth century enclosures had the effect of dispossessing small proprietors and casting small leaseholders and agricultural laborers adrift. In the Tudor period this had led to agrarian uprisings and specific, if ineffectual, attempts on the part of Crown and Parliament to curb the practice. In the eighteenth century, however, the situation had changed. Parliament, by virtue of the Revolution of 1688, now exercised almost complete control over the government, and Parliament was in turn controlled by the great landowners. Once the only hope of the victims of enclosure, the government was now the instrument of its beneficiaries. Thus, while the foundations of American agriculture were being laid by poor frontier farmers according to the democratic principles reflected by Thomas Jefferson, those of British agriculture were laid by a small but all-powerful landed aristocracy. "That by far the greater part of the island was owned by a comparatively small group of noblemen, gentlemen of family, and gentlemen in the making, is patent," is how one eminent British historian sums up the

toux, *Industrial Rev.*; Gonner, E. C. K., *Common Land and Enclosure*, London, 1912; Levy, H., *Large and Small Holdings*, Cambridge, 1911; Johnson, A. H., *The Disappearance of the Small Landowner*, Oxford, 1909; and Hasbach, W., *A History of the English Agricultural Labourer*, London, 1920.

situation in the early nineteenth century.[11] Landowning was now "mainly an aristocratic business"—[12] a far cry from the agrarian democracy on the American frontier.

The method of enclosure was decidedly undemocratic. It was carried out until 1845—that is, during its most active phase—by private act of Parliament. An individual or group that wished to enclose a given area would submit a petition to Parliament signed by the principal landowners and tithe-owners [13] interested in the project and representing a majority, not of the persons affected, but of the value of the properties involved. A bill embodying the petition would then be introduced, read, and referred to a committee, which would receive counterpetitions and hear evidence. Upon favorable report by the committee, the bill would then be passed by the House of Commons, sent to the Lords, and approved by the Crown. Having attained the status of public law, it empowered commissioners, named in its text, to proceed to the vicinity of the projected enclosure and carry it out according to plan. The principal landowner, or lord of the manor as he usually happened to be, was first permitted to incorporate in his estate such portions of the open fields and commons as he already owned and such additional portions as he desired to purchase. Next the tithe-owners were compensated, generally by allotments of land calculated to yield a revenue in cash or in kind equal to that of the existing tithes. Then the small owners of strips and the holders of rights to commons were paid off either with cash or with individual allotments of land.[14]

11. Clapham, *Econ. Hist. Mod. Brit.*, Vol. I, p. 98.
12. Curtler, *op. cit.*, p. 127. Cf. Ernle, *op. cit.*, pp. 141-144, 159-175.
13. Church taxes, generally paid in kind, for the support of local parish endowments. Cf. Ernle, *op. cit.*, Ch. XVI.
14. See Ernle, *op. cit.*, pp. 249-252 and the more detailed description of Curtler, *op. cit.*, pp. 152-169.

Fair and impartial on the surface, the procedure was from start to finish controlled by the wealthy landowners. They alone could afford the excessive costs of promotion and administration, of fees to lawyers, surveyors, commissioners, and parliamentary officials, of drainage, fencing, and road-building, of compensations to dispossessed proprietors and foreclosed leaseholders.[15] Against this array of caste, money, and protocol, the small owners and leaseholders were helpless. Their votes and counterpetitions, measured in terms of their possessions, were invariably outweighed by those of the wealthy minority. The latter framed the petitions, generally in secret, and dominated the Parliament and the parliamentary committees to which they were submitted. They chose the surveyors and solicitors, nominated the commissioners, and influenced their final dispensations. If justice stood in the way they were not averse from bribery and intimidation. Often the small allotments offered for sale to defray the costs of a large enclosure or as compensation to dispossessed owners were so expensive to fence and improve that the discouraged purchasers preferred to lapse into tenancy or migrate to the cities. Thus the "aristocratic business" of landowning was transacted until, by 1913, only 10 per cent of the total agricultural land of Britain was owned by those who occupied and cultivated it.[16]

There is no doubt that the enclosure movement facilitated the technical reforms that enabled British agriculture to keep pace with the demands of the rapidly increasing industrial population. It superimposed upon the archaic medieval sys-

15. See the statement of Lord Lincoln in introducing the General Enclosure Bill of 1845 "that in nineteen cases out of twenty, committees of this House sitting on private Bills neglected the rights of the poor." Hammond, J. L. and B., *The Village Labourer, 1760-1832*, London, 1927, p. 53.
16. Clapham, *op. cit.*, Vol. III, p. 534; Astor and Rowntree, *op. cit.*, p. 391.

tem of strip-cropping and common pasture a much more efficient organizational form, within which scientific methods of
farming could be employed and hitherto undreamed-of goals
of production achieved. It stimulated the accumulation of
capital, the introduction of farm machinery, soil conservation,
and the type of extensive cultivation best suited to grain, the
principal crop of the time. In so far as all of these improvements increased the productivity of British agriculture, both
per acre and per unit of labor, the enclosure movement
helped to create a labor surplus and resulting rural exodus.
It contributed more directly to the development of estate
farming on an unprecedented scale and to an equally unprecedented, and unparalleled, decline of the institution of small
farm ownership.[17]

The enclosures of the eighteenth and early nineteenth centuries caused much more social distress than those of the
Tudor period. There were frequent riots and rick-burnings in
the British countryside, and in 1830 an agricultural laborers'
revolt approached the dimensions of an insurrection.[18] That
the methods of enclosure were high-handed and lacking in
social justice is conceded even by those who minimize their
bad effects and defend them on economic grounds.[19] They

17. Notwithstanding the temporary increase of small owners during
the agricultural prosperity that accompanied the Napoleonic Wars.
The decline set in after 1815, and continued, with interrup-
tions, throughout the century. Cf. Curtler, *op. cit.*, pp. 238 ff.;
Davies, E., "The Small Landowner, 1780-1832, in the Light of
the Land Tax Assessments," *Economic History Review*, 1927,
Vol. I, pp. 87-113.

18. Hammond, J. L. and B., *The Village Labourer, 1760-1832*, Chs.
XI, XII.

19. E.g., Curtler, who, after reviewing the evidence of the Hammonds,
Johnson, Hasbach, Gonner, Ernle, and others, concludes that they
were "high-handed without a doubt" but "quite possible without
inflicting any distinct hardship on any one." . . . "All persons in
the parish who were interested in the enclosure should have been
consulted, but the larger proprietors and farmers were perfectly

inspired the romantic protest of *The Deserted Village;* and even Arthur Young, the leading proponent of large-scale farming, was moved to write a tract calling for more humane treatment of the rural poor and suggesting public allotments of waste land for their relief.[20] In like manner one of the leading modern British advocates of extensive, as opposed to small, holdings has declared: "For the balance of national advantage, it was necessary that the open fields should go, but . . . history . . . shows very clearly what the industrialization of agriculture has cost the English countryside, both in loss of economic opportunity for its workers, and in the loss of the sense of personal responsibility in the village community for its social institutions." [21] These were precisely the qualities that Thomas Jefferson considered most precious to democracy and best inculcated by the family farm. The British paid scant attention to them as they fenced off the land. "After 1790," says Lord Ernle, "no voice is raised against the movement on any other ground than the moral and social injury inflicted upon open-field farmers and commoners. The economic gain is admitted." [22] And the voice of protest was faint.

Measures taken to redress the grievances of the rural poor were almost as demoralizing as the method of enclosure. By the so-called "Speenhamland Act" of 1795, the wages of

convinced that enclosure was indispensable to agricultural progress, and knew very well too that there was a strong, and for the most part factious and ignorant, opposition to this desired improvement. But they were determined to carry their point, and at the same time deal justly (as the Acts and awards show) with all who had any legal claims." *Op. cit.*, pp. 155-156.

20. Young, Arthur, *An Inquiry into the Propriety of Applying Wastes to the Better Maintenance and Support of the Poor*, 1801. Hammond, *op. cit.*, pp. 82 ff.

21. Orwin, C. S., "Observations on the Open Fields," *Economic History Review*, 1938, Vol. VIII, p. 134.

22. Ernle, *op. cit.*, pp. 302-303.

agricultural laborers were tied to the price of bread, the difference between the prevailing wage and the bread price being made up out of parish poor rates. This practice, which spread through a large part of rural England, enabled the large employing farmers to evade the responsibility of paying a living wage and, as Trevelyan says of it, "most unjustly forced the small independent parishioner to help the big man, while at the same time it compelled the labourer to become a pauper even when he was in full work!" [23] It depressed agricultural wages, speeded the transfer of property from the small owner to the great, and filled the countryside with paupers until it was superseded by the scarcely more enlightened Poor Law of 1834, the inspiration of Dickens's *Oliver Twist*.[24] A General Enclosure Act of 1845 put an end to piecemeal enclosure by private acts, establishing permanent commissioners and regular allotments of ground for public recreation and poor relief. But the allotments for the poor were disappointingly small, and, in any case, the main wave of enclosures had spent itself. It was not until 1876 that an act with teeth in it brought the practice under effective public control.[25] By that time, as we shall see, a trend had started in the opposite direction, to regain lost ground and replace the small farmer on the land.

It is probably true, as modern authorities contend, that the evils of the enclosure movement have been exaggerated. Too much rural distress has been attributed to enclosures instead of to the industrial revolution, its real cause. It was the latter which infused agriculture with labor-saving techniques and

23. Trevelyan, G. M., *English Social History*, Longmans, Green & Co., Inc., New York, 1942, p. 469; cf. Curtler, *op. cit.*, pp. 241 ff.; Hammond, *op. cit.*, pp. 161 ff., and Chs. VIII, IX, X.

24. Trevelyan, *op. cit.*, p. 538; Clapham, *op. cit.*, Vol. I, pp. 127 ff., 132.

25. Curtler, *op. cit.*, Ch. XVIII. Public allotments totaled only 2,119 acres in 22 years. Clapham, *op. cit.*, Vol. II, p. 288.

swept away the small cottage industries that flourished in the countryside, simultaneously creating unemployment and removing the means of its local relief. The enclosure movement abetted these trends and took advantage of them, but it did not cause them. To this extent its leaders may be absolved of responsibility for the miseries of the rural people. The main and inescapable conclusions to be drawn here are that it was commercial rather than agrarian, and aristocratic rather than democratic, in character.

With the collapse of the war boom that followed Waterloo, rural conditions went from bad to worse. Small owners were dispossessed, leaseholders foreclosed, and agricultural laborers forced out of work faster than industry could re-employ them. The public conscience, not yet awake to what was happening, had provided no adequate means for tiding these people over in the transition. From their point of view, the Poor Law of 1834, which substituted the workhouse for direct, outdoor relief, was hardly an improvement on the Speenhamland system. They were cast upon their own resources: working on the road, scavenging, poaching to keep themselves and their families alive. Contemporary reports tell of "mothers dividing a farthing salt herring and a halfpenny worth of potatoes among a family of seven," of workmen's diets of bread and lard, skim milk, and rotten apples.[26] Riots were futile; poachers were greeted with spring guns and man traps and sentenced to penal colonies for snaring a few pheasant. Conditions were no better in the cities, but this thought gave no comfort to the rural poor. A wedge was being driven between those who owned the land and those who labored upon it.

The wedge was hammered in by a series of blows that fell upon it during the first half of the nineteenth century until

26. Curtler, *op. cit.*, pp. 272 ff.; Hammond, *op. cit.*, Chs. VIII, IX.

it split the solid agrarian front. The final and most decisive blow was the repeal of the Corn Laws in 1846. This was the second of the two great measures whereby the British converted their country into the workshop of the world and subordinated agriculture to its needs. Enclosure transformed subsistence farming into commercial farming under capitalist management. Free trade enabled British manufacturers to take advantage of their tremendous lead on all competitors for the world market: it promised their customers a means of exchange for British industrial products and it provided their labor with cheap food, which meant low wages. Enclosure had been planned and executed by the landed aristocracy that had controlled local government through the county courts and dominated Parliament as a closed corporation for over a century. The same oligarchy, or "squirearchy" as it has been more appropriately called, fought free trade tooth and nail.

How could it have had its way so arbitrarily in the one case and yet have been defeated in the other? The answer lies partly in the democratic currents that had at last begun to break the barriers of caste and custom, partly in the industrial revolution from which they stemmed. From the apparent contradiction one immediate conclusion may be drawn. Both enclosure and free trade were calculated to maximize the supply of foodstuffs in the British Isles, the one by more efficient domestic production, the other by importation. That the British public should have supported two measures so much alike in economic purpose yet so unlike in political significance shows the extent to which they had come to think of their agriculture as a source of food and national wealth rather than as the mainstay of a particular state of society or way of life.

Democracy, either in the sense of popular sovereignty or

of equal social and economic opportunity, had made little headway in Great Britain up to the end of the Napoleonic Wars. In the sense of a rule of law before which all men were equal, it had long existed, and in fuller measure than anywhere else in the world. During the seventeenth and eighteenth centuries it had appeared here and there in speculative writings and religious tracts. But the beginning of the nineteenth century found British government, like British landowning, "mainly an aristocratic business." Society was rigidly stratified and economic opportunity distributed according to wealth. "The most ordinary knowledge of the commonest events shows us that in 1800 the government of England was essentially aristocratic," says Dicey, "and that the class which, though never despotic, was decidedly dominant, was the class of landowners and of large merchants; and that the social condition, the feelings and convictions of Englishmen in 1800 were even more aristocratic than were English political institutions." [27] The House of Lords, in which sat four hundred hereditary peers of the realm, thirty Anglican bishops, and the elective peers of Scotland and Ireland, was a landowners' monopoly. The House of Commons was only slightly less so. Here were represented 203 towns or boroughs and 40 counties or shires, each by two members. The franchise was restricted in each type of electoral district: in the county, to freeholders owning land to the annual rental value of 40 shillings; in the borough, according to a variety of property qualifications and the whim of the controlling peer or magnate. Many of the boroughs had been created generations ago and no longer bore any relation, save that of corruption, to the present distribution of the population. These so-called "rotten boroughs" were nearly all controlled by peers, who bought and sold their seats in a brisk traffic

27. Dicey, A. V., *Law and Opinion in England*, London, 1940, p. 48.

and thus extended their influence into the House of Commons. Others were owned by wealthy commoners. So commonplace had the practice become that the Treasury thought it wise to control a bloc of borough seats in order to assure the party in power a safe margin in the Commons. It has been estimated that the majority of the House of Commons was elected by less than 15,000 voters, and that no fewer than 357 members owed their seats to no more than 154 individuals, most of them nobles, and all of them wealthy.[28] Here was a system of government, both local and national, that fitted the classic definition of oligarchy, not democracy.

Had it survived intact until 1846, it is difficult to see how the Corn Laws could ever have been repealed. But by that time industrialism had weakened its foundations, and from the cities rather than from the farms and villages had come the agitation for political and social reform that ushered in modern British democracy. The American and French revolutions, the doctrines of Thomas Paine, Cobbett, Bentham, and Robert Owen, the new high tariff of 1815, the Peterloo Massacre of 1819,[29] recurring depression, all these and many other factors must be reckoned in the process. Basically, however, it was the industrial revolution, filling the cities with masses of factory workers, unprotected against inhuman working conditions, insecure in their employment, and unrepresented in government, that brought democracy to Britain. Even though they lacked the franchise, the pressure of these masses for relief and reform at length became irresistible. In 1802, and again in 1819, it had borne fruit in feeble attempts at factory legislation. In 1832 it produced a substantial re-

28. Dietz, F. C., *A Political and Social History of England*, New York, 1933, p. 496, and Ch. XXIII, *passim*.
29. In which a crowd of demonstrators was dispersed by cavalry, with several deaths and numerous casualties.

form of Parliament and, in 1833, the first of a long series of acts regulating conditions of labor in industry.[30]

Although, by modern standards, the Reform Bill of 1832 was a minimal compromise with democracy, it paved the way for the repeal of the Corn Laws in 1846. Lord Grey told the king that it was an "aristocratical" measure, designed to save the constitution from more radical change, and it was only on this basis, and after a savage battle, that he was able to get it past the House of Lords. Yet it was just enough to tilt the scales in favor of free trade when that test came. The bill extended the franchise and the process of popular election, but not far. The franchise was given to citizens of boroughs paying ten pounds' rent, and in the counties to long-term leaseholders and copyholders paying 10 pounds' rent and short-term leaseholders paying 50 pounds' rent. It freed some 200 seats in the House of Commons from rotten borough control and made them subject to popular election, and it revised the distribution of representation in favor of the cities. It did not establish equal electoral districts or institute the secret ballot; it fell a long way short of universal suffrage; but it did admit to the franchise and to the process of government the more prosperous elements of the middle class. Through them, and through the redistribution of borough seats, it enhanced the political power of the manufacturing interest.

Free trade now had friends in Parliament, and with their support the disciples of Adam Smith and Ricardo launched a crusade for repeal. Seldom in history have theoretical ideas found such formidable practical champions as the ideas of the

30. For the circumstances leading up to the repeal of the Corn Laws, see Trevelyan, *British History in the Nineteenth Century*; Dietz, *op. cit.*, esp. Chs. XXIII, XXIV; Dicey, A. V., *Law and Opinion in England*, Lectures III-VI; Barnes, D. G., *A History of the English Corn Laws*, London, 1930, Chs. VII-XII.

economists found in Richard Cobden, Huskisson, and Sir
Robert Peel. For seven years (1838-1845) Cobden's Anti-
Corn Law League stumped England, carrying the argument
into every industrial center and rural hamlet. Poor crops,
high food prices, and industrial depressions aided their efforts, especially from 1838 to 1842. Trade unionism sprang
up in the cities, and the Chartists began to agitate their six
points, all but the last of which were eventually to become
the law, and the last the custom, of the land: universal suffrage, secret ballot, equal electoral districts, payment of
Members of Parliament, abolition of property qualifications,
and annual Parliaments. The urban masses did not need
much convincing that free trade was in their interest. And
in the country, enclosures, hunger, and unemployment produced almost as many converts among the poor. Enclosure
had thinned the ranks of the independent freeholders who
might have stood with the landlords against repeal.[31] Economic theory, humanitarianism, and the self-interest of the
commercial and industrial population, which now outnumbered the agricultural,[32] daily strengthened the free trade
cause.

At length, Sir Robert Peel, leader of the Tory majority,
elected to maintain the Corn Laws, became convinced that
they should be repealed. An Irish famine in 1845 and a
simultaneous spell of wet weather that ruined British crops
moved him to action. In a parliamentary struggle, as dra-

31. How far they had been reduced in number may be judged by the
fact that in 1846 not more than 15 per cent of the total land was
occupied by its owners. Clapham gives this as the minimum figure
for 1831. In view of the long-run trend, it seems a generous maximum for 1846. (*Econ. Hist.*, Vol. I, pp. 102-105.)

32. Occupational returns for the census of 1851 showed 1,790,000
employed in agriculture as compared with 2,500,000 (including
376,000 unskilled laborers) in manufacturing and building and
250,000 in mining. Clapham, *op. cit.*, Vol. II, p. 24.

matic in character as it was momentous in consequence, he carried the day for repeal. The Duke of Wellington, who nevertheless supported him in his *volte-face*, maintained that "rotten potatoes . . . put Peel in his d—d fright," others, that it had "rained away the Corn Laws." [33] Peel himself attributed his conversion to Cobden. He had split his party and brooked the charge of treason. As soon as the final vote was taken, he resigned from office and retired to private life. In the perspective of history it seems obvious that he had chosen to follow the popular majority outside of Parliament rather than the party majority within.

The British people turned against the Corn Laws in full realization of their significance to British agriculture. For nearly two centuries the laws had stood upon the statute books, protecting and encouraging domestic producers of grain. Behind their shelter, the landed aristocracy, that controlled British agriculture, had put through the enclosure movement. But in proportion as the enclosures reduced the number of producers, the laws tended to assume the aspect of class legislation that kept rents and food prices over the heads of the poor and benefited ever fewer, wealthier, and more exalted people. The pamphleteers of the Anti-Corn Law League made the most of this impression, denouncing the farmers and landlords as enemies of the people. The latter countered by forming the Agricultural Protection Society for the United Kingdom of Great Britain and Ireland, and engaging the League in an epic of invective. [34] This was the propagandist version of the more serious, though no less intense, debate that raged in Parliament through the winter

33. Cf. Trevelyan, *British History in the Nineteenth Century*, pp. 270 ff.
34. For the tone and substance of the argument on both sides as reflected in contemporary pamphlets, see Barnes, *op. cit.*, esp. Chs. X and XI.

and spring of 1846. There, too, the same lines were drawn: urban commercialism and industrialism, supported by a rising tide of democracy, versus agrarian aristocracy—exactly the reverse of Jefferson's scheme. The theme of the agrarians throughout the debate was that repeal would ruin British agriculture utterly and completely. It does not matter that Cobden and his followers prophesied agricultural prosperity under free trade, that for a number of years after repeal their prophecy came true, or that, in the long run, many of the agrarians' worst fears were justified. The point is that they stated their case against repeal as against the doom of agriculture and the agrarian way of life, and that the British people heard the case and dismissed it in favor of cheaper food and greater commercial opportunity.

The political and social theory upon which the agrarians based their case was the opposite of Thomas Jefferson's. It was most forcefully stated by Benjamin Disraeli, who came to their defense in the Commons and by his dialectical skill quickly made himself their leader in the parliamentary debate. Disraeli had taken his first seat in the House of Commons in 1837 as a borough member from Maidstone, Kent, and a staunch admirer of Sir Robert Peel. In 1841 he had been returned from the borough of Shrewsbury in a great Tory victory led by Peel. When the latter set about forming a ministry, Disraeli applied to him for office but was politely rebuffed. He did not forget this blow to his very considerable vanity, and when Peel began to show signs of weakening on the issue of free trade, Disraeli turned savagely against him. Consistency and party loyalty were on the side of Disraeli. He was the representative of a rural constituency, pledged to protection. His party had won its majority on the promise to maintain the Corn Laws. No doubt vanity, ambition, and opportunism led him to make the most of consistency. At all events, as soon as Peel revealed his intentions, Disraeli unleashed at him a series of philippics so pointed and personal that they nearly resulted in a duel, and so forceful that they were almost as potent a factor in splitting the Tories as the action of the Prime Minister himself.[35] The speeches made a national sensation. They were the last desperate hope of the agrarian protectionists and, as such, a mirror of their ideas.

Like Jefferson's, Disraeli's interest in agriculture was political and social rather than economic. "I will never commit myself upon this great question to petty economic details," he had told his constituents in 1843; ". . . what I want, and what I wish to secure, and what, as far as my energies go, I will secure, is the preponderance of the landed interest."

Gentlemen, when I talk of the preponderance of the landed interest, do not for a moment suppose that I mean merely the preponderance of "squires of high degree," that, in fact, I am thinking only of justices of the peace. My thought wanders farther than a lordly tower or a manorial hall. I am looking in that phrase, in using that very phrase, to what I consider the vast majority of the English nation. I do not undervalue the mere superiority of the landed classes; on the contrary, I think it a most necessary element of political power and national civilisation; but I am looking to the population of our innumerable villages, to the crowds in our rural towns: aye, and I mean even something more than that by the landed interest—I mean that estate . . . of the poor, the great estate of the Church, which has, before this time, secured our liberty, and may, for aught I know, still secure our civilisation. I mean, also, by the landed interest, that great judicial fabric, that great building up of our laws and manners which is, in fact,

35. For a full account of Disraeli's part in the debate see Monypenny, Wm. F., *The Life of Benjamin Disraeli*, New York, 1913, Vol. II, esp. Chs. VIII, X, XI. The episode of the averted duel is described on p. 379. For text of Disraeli's speeches in the debate, see *Selected Speeches of the Earl of Beaconsfield*, T. E. Kebbel, ed., London, 1882, Vol. I, pp. 35-173; for full report of the debate, *Hansard's Parliamentary Debates*, Third Series, Vols. LXXXIII-LXXXVII.

the ancient polity of the realm, and the ancient constitution of the realm—those ancient institutions which we Conservatives are bound to uphold—which you sent us to Parliament to uphold. . . .[36]

The English constitution consisted of more than "Queen, Lords and Commons." Trial by jury was just as important a part, and trial by jury "arises out of your landed tenure of property." Destroy agriculture and you destroy that tenure of property; destroy that tenure of property and you destroy all those institutions.

That was the "most important point, which has never yet been properly brought before any deliberative assembly." Church, state, the "great fabric of judicial rights," the "traditionary manners and associations which spring out of the land," all would collapse with agriculture. He preferred to take "the only broad and only safe line—namely, that what we ought to uphold is, the preponderance of the landed interest. . . ."[37] "The landed interest should be the basis of our political and social system."[38] It had seen England through many revolutions. It had even restored the nation to itself after Cromwell.

Shall I tell you how it was that the nation returned to itself, and Old England, after the deluge, was seen rising above the waters? This was the reason—because during all that fearful revolution you never changed the tenure of your landed property. That, I think, gentlemen, proves my case; and if we have baffled a wit like Oliver Cromwell, let us not be staggered even before Mr. Cobden! The acres remained; the estates remained. The generations changed: the Puritan father died, and the Cavalier son came into his place, and, backed by that power and influence, the nation reverted to the ancient principles of the realm. And this, gentlemen, is the reason why you have seen an outcry raised against your

36. Beaconsfield, *Speeches*, Vol. I, pp. 48-49.
37. *Ibid.*, pp. 52-53.
38. *Ibid.*, p. 55.

Corn Laws. Your Corn Laws are merely the outwork of a great system fixed and established upon your territorial property, and the only object the Leaguers have in making themselves masters of the outwork is that they may easily overcome the citadel.[39]

Far from defending agriculture in the name of democracy, the leader of the agrarians was imputing democratic motives to the free traders in order to discredit them.

Time and again, as he pressed his attack on Peel, Disraeli reverted to these fundamental views. The secret of England's greatness was her "territorial constitution that has invested the possession of land with an honour peculiar to itself." [40]

I repeat what I have repeated before, that in this country there are special reasons why we should not only maintain the balance between the two branches of our national industry, but why we should give a preponderance . . . to the agricultural branch; and the reason is, because in England we have a territorial constitution.[41]

He devoted much time to sarcastic appraisals of Peel's party record, which drew cheers and laughter from the disaffected Tories, but he invariably returned to that main point. We stress it here, not because it was decisive in the debate, which it was not, but because it reveals so clearly the political and social spirit of British agrarianism. Democracy was not at stake in the repeal of the Corn Laws, indeed it was hardly relevant to the argument. The free traders denied that agriculture was at stake. The Tories had made it seem to be and had defended it in the name of monarchy and aristocracy. That is as close as the British came to establishing a generic connection between agrarianism and democracy in 1846.

After all the excitement of the protectionists, the immediate effects of repeal were an anticlimax. It was, says Tre-

39. *Ibid.*, pp. 56-57.
40. *Ibid.*, p. 136.
41. *Ibid.*, p. 142.

velyan, "a political triumph for Manchester and for the urban population; and it certainly helped industry. But it effected no immediate economic or social revolution. The cities belonged to democracy, but the country-side was still in the hands of the landlord class, and of their deputies and allies the tenant-farmers, whose affairs were much more flourishing in the 'sixties than they had been a generation before." [42] The full impact of free trade was not felt by British farmers until the seventies, when the rapid development of railways, steamship lines, and refrigeration brought American, Dominion, and Argentine wheat and meat flooding into the domestic market. Then, at last, Disraeli's fears were justified. Agriculture entered a twenty-year depression, the rural exodus gathered momentum, and the agricultural population sank to new low levels. [43]

Again the cry for protection was raised, and again denied. In 1894 a Royal Commission, appointed to investigate the agricultural depression, heard evidence from all over rural Britain and from every type and class of farmer. The burden of this evidence shows that whereas the earlier phases of the depression were largely attributed to poor crops at home, this one was almost unanimously blamed on competition from abroad. "Only better seasons and improved prices can, it is argued, restore agriculture to a flourishing condition in this district," reported one of the commissioners. "As the seasons are beyond control, the question remains, By what means can improved prices be established? The answer I received, in

42. Trevelyan, *English Social History*, p. 534.
43. From 1881 to 1901, while the total population increased from 34.8 million to 41.4 million and the working population from 12.7 to 16.3 million, the number of persons employed in agriculture declined from 1.6 to 1.4 million, or from 12.5 per cent to 8.6 per cent of the working population. See *Statistical Abstract for the United Kingdom*, 1938, pp. 4-5, 128-129.

nine cases out of ten, in all parts of this district may be summed up in one word—'protection.' " [44]

In almost every reply I received, the chief causes of depression are attributed to low prices resulting from foreign competition and bad seasons, with consequent failure of corn and hay crops. For the latter no remedy but patience can be found, but the former is considered removable by a change in the fiscal system which would force the foreigner to pay a corresponding tax to that borne by the producer of home-grown corn and hay, by the makers of cheese, butter, etc., and by those engaged in every agricultural industry, which is now severely handicapped by the preference given to the foreigner.[45]

But new reform bills had enfranchised the factory workers in 1867, and the agricultural laborers in 1884; these two classes saw eye-to-eye on the price of bread, and protection was not forthcoming. Joseph Chamberlain's scheme of imperial preferences and protective tariffs was defeated in a free trade landslide in 1906. Not until the world depression of 1932 threatened the entire British economy with collapse was protection resorted to, and then in the interest of national recovery and security rather than of the agrarian way of life.

The farm population of Great Britain was now barely 6 per cent of the working population. It had never been able to convince the British democracy, whose rise accompanied its decline, of its special sociological claims to protection. Most of it—the agricultural laborers—did not wish to. For the rest—the minority of landlords and independent producers— the facts speak for themselves. They had repeatedly stated

44. Great Britain. Royal Commission on Agriculture, *Reports by Dr. W. Fream on the Andover District of Hampshire and the Maidstone District of Kent*, 1894, p. 16. This report is appended to minutes of hearings of commission in Great Britain. *Reports of Commissions, etc.*, 1894, Vol. XVI, Parts 1-3, *Agriculture*, Part 1.
45. Royal Comm. on Agr., *Report by Mr. Jabez Turner on the Frome District of Somerset*, p. 13. *Loc. cit.*

those claims, and repeatedly they had been rejected. Disraeli had led a lost cause. "The repeal of the Corn Laws was the first decisive step in the policy of sacrificing the rural life of England to a one-sided and exaggerated industrial development," lamented his biographer in 1913.[46] And in 1943, while the National Agricultural Jefferson Bicentenary Committee was bestowing its tributes on the founder of American agriculture, a leader of the modern British agrarians proclaimed:

> Disraeli understood the English character and the foundation of its greatness, and he spoke the voice of England. I would have England turn again to Disraeli for inspiration, for that would be to return again to the land.[47]

The prospects that the lost cause would be revived and won were slim. From the moment they began, the rural exodus and the disappearance of the independent family farmer, the "sturdy yeoman" of English tradition, had been deplored by intellectuals and reformers. Arthur Young, as we have seen, had reversed himself to the extent of pleading for public allotments for the dispossessed, pinning his faith on "the magic of property" and declaring: "A man will love his country the better even for a pig." [48] *The Deserted Village* has become an international symbol of agrarian reform. In 1821 William Cobbett had written in the *Political Register*:

> I hold a return to *small farms* to be *absolutely necessary* to a restoration to anything like an English community; and I am quite sure, that the ruin of the present race of farmers, generally, is a necessary preliminary to this. . . . The life of the husbandman cannot be that of *a gentleman* without injury to society at large. When farmers become *gentlemen* their labourers become slaves. . . . It is in those States of America, where the farmer is only the

46. Monypenny, *op. cit.*, Vol. II, p. 404.
47. Stapledon, Sir R. George, *Disraeli and the New Age*, London, 1943, p. 5.
48. Cf. Hammond, *op. cit.*, p. 84.

first labourer that all the domestic virtues are to be found, and all that public-spirit and that valour, which are the safeguards of American independence, freedom, and happiness. . . . Take England throughout, *three farms have been turned into one within fifty years.* . . . Instead of families of small farmers with all their exertions, all their decency of dress and of manners, and all their scrupulousness as to character, we have *families of paupers,* with all the improvidence and wrecklessness [*sic*] belonging to an irrevocable sentence of poverty for life.[49]

John Stuart Mill took up the refrain in a series of articles on Ireland in the *Morning Chronicle* in the winter of 1846-47[50] and repeated it in his *Principles of Political Economy.*[51] Although these men did not attempt to prove the agrarian-democratic equation, they emphasized the same social and moral values of agriculture and of family farming as Jefferson.

At length Jesse Collings, an agrarian reformer whose slogan was "Three Acres and a Cow," carried their arguments into Parliament. The agricultural depression of the seventies and eighties added fuel to his fire. Joseph Chamberlain came to his support, and in 1882 an act was passed providing that a small proportion of the land reserved for the poor of each parish should be made available to them in the form of allotments.[52] Allotments, in British usage, were

49. Quoted in *ibid.,* pp. 212-213.
50. MacMinn, N., Hainds, J. R., and McCrimmon, J. McN., *Bibliography of the Published Writings of John Stuart Mill,* Evanston, 1945, pp. 60-67. Mill used the peasant small holdings of Switzerland and France as examples of the thrift, industry, and land improvement they would bring about in Ireland.
51. Levy, H., *Large and Small Holdings,* pp. 73 ff.; Clapham, *op. cit.,* Vol. III, p. 104; Mill, J. S., *Principles of Political Economy,* 6th ed., London, 1865, pp. 164-193.
52. Details of the allotments and small-holdings movement from Curtler, *op. cit.,* Chs. XIX-XXII; Venn, *op. cit.,* Chs. V, VI; Levy, *op. cit.,* Chs. III, VII, VIII; Jebb, L., *The Small Holdings of*

small plots of land, generally not over half an acre, held and cultivated by nonagricultural as well as agricultural laborers as part-time aids to their household economies. The setting aside of laborers' allotments had begun with the early enclosure acts around 1801 and had continued on a more or less voluntary basis until the depression discouraged it. The purpose of the act of 1882 was to revive the practice by making it a public responsibility of the local parishes. But the parish authorities found one reason or another for evading it and the act was a failure.

Collings and his friends now turned their attention to small holdings, tracts of from 1 to 50 acres, intended as full-time subsistence farms. A special committee, of which he and Joseph Chamberlain became members, was formed and, after hearing evidence, reported that witnesses "of all classes and of all opinions" believed that "an increase of small cultivators would be a distinct national and social advantage."

All agree that the existence of a numerous and prosperous peasantry is a condition of national safety, and that the more general distribution of ownership in land, would lead to the security of property, and to the contentment of the population.

There is similar unanimity as to the effect upon character of the responsibility involved in the secure possession of small holdings.

Whether as owners or as tenants, the class of small holders is distinguished for industry, thrift, and other civic virtues. Where facilities exist for the creation of such holdings, the ordinary la-

England, London, 1907, Ch. IX; Clapham, *op. cit.*, Vol. III, pp. 101-120; Orwin, C. S., and Darke, W. F., *Back to the Land*, Oxford, 1935, *passim*; Ashby, Arthur W., *Allotments and Small Holdings in Oxfordshire*, Oxford, 1917, esp. Part I, Ch. II, and Part II, Ch. VII; Orwin, C. S., and Peel, M. A., *The Tenure of Agricultural Land*, Cambridge, 1925, *passim*; Great Britain, Agricultural Tribunal of Investigation, *Final Report*, 1924; Great Britain, Commissioner for the Special Areas, *Report of the Committee of Enquiry into Land Settlement*, 1939; Astor and Rowntree, *British Agriculture*, Ch. XVIII. Particular sources cited below.

bourer has encouragement and hope; he sees an opportunity for getting his foot on the first step of the ladder by which he may win a better position. Without this hope "he is only a bird of passage; there is no national sentiment in his heart. In the absence of a home a man has very little to look for."

The prospect of improvement for the thrifty and industrious labourer is a matter of the highest social importance. It is the chief means by which a remedy can be found for that migration from the country into the towns, which has to some extent depopulated the rural districts, and has, at the same time, intensified the competition for employment in the manufacturing towns.

The committee was not so sure of the economic advantages as it was of the social. It looked with favor upon the "magic of ownership, referred to by Arthur Young, which turns sand into gold," but was bound to report that "the ambition of the rural population is rather in the direction of small tenancies than of cultivating ownership." [53]

On the strength of this report, the Small Holdings Act of 1892 was passed, empowering county councils to acquire land for sale or lease in small holdings of 1 to 50 acres. Clapham calls the act a "blank failure," [54] which indeed it was. Only 59 small holdings were sold and 185 leased under its terms in 15 years, the whole comprising a mere 880 acres. [55] The results, in these few cases satisfied expectations, but good land was scarce, mortgage requirements were high, times were hard, and, most significant of all, the actual demand for small holdings was slight. Collings was not daunted. "Nations may have brilliant epochs—more or less long-

---

53. Great Britain, *Reports from Committees*, XVII, 1890, "Report from the Select Committee on Small Holdings," pp. iii-v.
54. *Op. cit.*, III, p. 106.
55. To be exact, 881½ acres. Figures are those taken by Curtler from the Report of the Board of Agriculture, 1908, and given by him in *op. cit.*, p. 296. Clapham, *op. cit.*, Vol. III, p. 106, takes the total acreage of 812 acres from Jebb, *Small Holdings*, pp. 331-333, an earlier (1907) and less reliable source.

continued—of commercial prosperity, with vast accumulations of money wealth," he wrote in 1906, "but their strength, virility, permanence, and resisting power must ever depend on a numerous rural population." [56] And private property, " 'the magic of ownership'—whether of field, farm, wife, child, or any other possession, will ever remain the natural and the best means to disclose a man's capacity and to spur his activity." [57] But the imagination of the British people had followed Mahan and Kipling along the paths of empire, sea power, and world politics, far afield from their own countryside. Allotments accumulated, mostly without government intervention, but the small-holdings movement struggled on without much success or popular support.

An act of 1908 which abandoned proprietorship for tenancy and gave the county councils compulsory powers to requisition land created something over 14,000 small holdings by the outbreak of the First World War, only 2 per cent of them owned, and most of them falling far short of full-time subsistence enterprises. [58] Further legislation of the same sort followed during the war and in 1919, 1926, and 1931. Somewhat under the influence of "arcadian propaganda," 50,000 veterans applied for small holdings after the war, but by 1922 only 17,000 had actually settled on them. [59] Even with the national government financing them as a means of unemployment relief in the distressed areas during the blackest days of the world depression, they did not take hold. "In the minds of those who started the land settlement movement," reported a parliamentary investigating committee in 1939, "it is probable that the social aspect was as

56. Collings, J., *Land Reform*, Longmans, Green & Co., Inc., London, 1906, p. x.
57. *Ibid.*, p. 422.
58. Venn, *op. cit.*, Ch. VI; Curtler, *op. cit.*, pp. 299 ff.
59. Venn, *op. cit.*, pp. 126-136.

important as the financial or economic. They wished to re-move the men and their families from the hopeless and de-grading conditions of continued unemployment in depressed areas." Nevertheless, the best the committee could claim was "that while nearly half of the would-be settlers had given up . . . and gone back to their old homes, sometimes with unfavourable stories of the land settlement schemes, a sur-prising number of those that remained, and often their wives, expressed satisfaction with their new surroundings, sometimes with enthusiasm." [60] And it ended its report with a pro-nouncement in favor of co-operative farms instead of indi-vidual small holdings.[61]

It is true that earlier acts had recruited small-holders from applicants with previous agricultural experience, while the one under investigation, the Special Areas (Development and Improvement) Act of 1934, undertook the more difficult task of resettling—and training—miners and industrial workers. Nevertheless, by March 31, 1939, only 1,479 holdings had been developed under its terms, of which 389 were vacant, and upon which only 693 families had been settled.[62] With-out a doubt great benefits accrued to those who made a suc-cess of the venture, but with the unemployed counted in the millions, they did not add up to an impressive total. The re-sults of this latest promotion of small holdings recapitulated those of the entire movement. From 1885, when it began, to 1939, the total number of agricultural holdings over 1 acre in England and Wales declined from 452,988 to 361,663. Whereas farms of 100 to 300 acres decreased very little (from 67,024 to 66,032), and those of 50 to 100 acres actually in-creased from 54,937 to 61,348, and although farms of over

60. Great Britain, Commissioner for the Special Areas, *Report of the Committee of Enquiry into Land Settlement*, p. 130.
61. *Ibid.*, p. 134.
62. *Ibid.*, pp. 7-11.

300 acres decreased from 16,608 to 11,864, the most considerable decrease occurred in holdings of 1 to 5 acres
(114,273 to 61,384, or 46 per cent), while those of 5 to 50
acres decreased from 201,146 to 161,035, or 20 per cent.[63]
The point of these statistics is that the decrease was greatest
in precisely those small holdings that the state was trying to
increase. Once more we should make allowance for the small-
holders who were able to climb the "agricultural ladder";
but so far as promoting a return to the land or a revival of
family farming was concerned, the policy was not a success.

As to occupying ownership, a prime qualification of the
American family farm, it had risen from around 11 per cent
of all agricultural holdings and 10 per cent of the land in
1913 to 17 per cent of the holdings and 36 per cent of the
land in 1927.[64] In 1938 the Ministry of Agriculture fixed the
proportion of land owned by its occupiers at one-third.[65]
The First World War, heavy taxes, and the depression had
brought about a substantial transfer of land in favor of small
owners; but in contrast to the 75 per cent of French farmers
who owned their own farms in 1929,[66] and the 58 per cent
of American farmers who owned theirs in 1935,[67] the British
total of 17 per cent was exceedingly small. Moreover, while
the British figure represented the peak of owner-occupancy
in that country during the past century, the American figure
represented the lowest point in our own history. Tenant
farming on a relatively large scale remained the predomi-

63. Figures from Venn, *op. cit.*, p. 110, and Great Britain, Ministry
    of Agriculture and Fisheries, *Agricultural Statistics*, 1939, Part I,
    p. 43. Most of the decline in the 5-50 acre group was in units of
    5-20 acres. Cf. Orwin and Darke, *op. cit.*, pp. 44-47.
64. These official estimates from Venn, *op. cit.*, pp. 110-113, are ac-
    cepted by Clapham, *op. cit.*, Vol. III, pp. 117 and 534.
65. Astor and Rowntree, *op. cit.*, p. 391.
66. Yates, *Food Production in Western Europe*, pp. 276-277.
67. *Farm Tenancy*. Report of the President's Committee, February,
    1937, p. 3.

nant pattern of British agriculture. A national rededication to peasant proprietorship and the agrarian way of life was not in sight.

No one has explained this national attitude better than Jesse Collings, to whom it was a cause of deep regret. "Unhappily," he wrote in 1906, "the mass of the people of this country have been so long cut off from any connection with the land that they have ceased to regard agriculture as a subject which specially affects them. They regard it simply as one among many industries, instead of as being the root of all others. . . ."[68] Cut off from the land they had been, by enclosures, industrialism, free trade, and their own predilections for commerce and empire. And though they cherished their countryside and rural traditions as few other people, and though hardly a season failed to produce a fresh crop of agrarian literature,[69] the fate of the small-holdings movement was probably a more reliable measure of the likelihood of an agrarian revival than the voices of the revivalists.

Great Britain has long been compelled by the exigencies of her international position to give more heed to her economists and her national interest than to her agrarians or any other particular section of her political or economic society. A chronic depression in agricultural prices forced the government's hand to credit and marketing legislation in 1923 and a few import quotas in the following years. When in 1932 it came to the rescue of agriculture with a full repertoire of tariffs, import quotas, subsidies, and price controls,[70] it did

68. Collings, *Land Reform*, p. xiv.
69. E.g., Massingham, H. J., ed., *The Natural Order: Essays in the Return to Husbandry*, London, 1945; Stapledon, Sir R. George, *Disraeli and the New Age*.
70. For details see Astor and Rowntree, *British Agriculture*, *passim*; *Agriculture in the Twentieth Century*, Oxford, 1939, esp. pp. 51-87; Astor and Murray, K. A. H., *The Planning of Agriculture*, Oxford, 1933; Rowntree, etc., *The Agricultural Dilemma*, London, 1935; Venn, *op. cit.*, Ch. XXIV.

so by necessity rather than conviction. The national economy was in a state of collapse. Monthly unemployment lists ran close to 3,000,000.[71] Foreign trade had been throttled, hostile dictatorships were in the making, and war loomed on the horizon. With the advent of the Second World War, all considerations of ways of life and patterns of society were forgotten in the greatest crisis in the nation's history. Under the direction of the Ministry of Agriculture and the decentralized control of county and district War Agriculture Committees, old pastures, village greens, golf courses—every square inch that was not needed for military purposes—were plowed up and put to crops. By these means Britain increased her arable crop land from 11,800,000 acres in 1939 to 18,000,000 in 1943, and her food production from roughly a third to 70 per cent of domestic requirements.[72]

This extraordinary accomplishment, made possible by the labor of women, children, soldiers, war prisoners, and all sorts of volunteers, by the use of agricultural machinery on an unprecedented scale,[73] and by an equally unprecedented economic mobilization of the state, gave the advocates of agrarian revival and economic self-sufficiency a new lease on life. They hoped and urged, after victory, that wartime technical improvements be continued, domestic food production kept high, and a systematic effort to increase the farm population, particularly family farmers, be undertaken by the government; and they rested their case primarily on strategic

71. *Statistical Abstract for the United Kingdom, 1939*, p. 132.
72. Easterbrook, Laurence F., *British Agriculture*, London, 1944, pp. 23-44; Menzies-Kitchin, A. W., *The Future of British Farming*, pp. 30-35; British Information Services, *The British Farmer's Battle and Victory*, pp. 6-7, 11, 17.
73. The Women's Land Army grew from 9,000 in 1940 to over 75,000 in 1943, and the number of tractors in use on British farms from 55,000 in 1939 to 165,000 in 1943. *Ibid.*, pp. 29-31.

security and the social, though not specifically the demo-cratic, virtues of agriculture.[74]

There was general agreement among those concerned with British agricultural policy as to the need for technical im-provements and rural rehabilitation.[75] Technical progress had been slow until the war speeded it up, and modes of living had remained virtually unchanged since the hard times of the 1880's. "It is a hard fact that rural England, notwith-standing all its variety and beauty and the opportunities which it affords for employment in sunshine and fresh air such as few industrial workers know, lags far behind any well-administered industrial area in all that it can offer alike in economic advancement, in creature comforts, and in social amenities for its dwellers." So reported a committee of inves-tigators which conducted a rural survey during the war under the auspices of the Agricultural Economics Research Institute of Oxford University.

Living conditions in any beautiful village compare most un-favourably with those on any municipal housing estate. Houses themselves are too often damp, dark, ill ventilated, and ill found. Piped water is almost unknown in most cottages, and in hundreds of villages there are no supplies even to stand-pipes in the streets. It follows, of course, that internal sanitation and arrangements for sewage disposal are equally rare. Slops are emptied in the garden, baths are non-existent, and the outside privy-vault is uni-versal. The same unfavourable contrast may be made in other public services—gas, electricity, scavenging, etc.

In economic opportunity, too, the country dweller finds himself in many ways at a disadvantage. His children may suffer from the handicap of inferior education. The one-room school, in which children of all ages from 3 to 11 are instructed by one school-

74. Cf. Stapledon, *Disraeli and the New Age*, pp. 67 ff.; Massingham, *The Natural Order*, esp. Chs. IV-VI, XII; Fordham, M., *The Land and Life*, London, 1942, *passim*.

75. In this connection, see the review of opinion in Menzies-Kitchin, *op. cit.*, Ch. II.

mistress and perhaps a pupil-teacher, is still to be found, and no amount of devotion on their part can overcome the difficulties of teaching in such conditions. Senior schools for older children involve journeys by road or rail, with attendant drawbacks which are accentuated for any who may be selected to proceed to higher education.

Conditions of employment in agriculture likewise suffered in comparison; the whole prospect drove people out of farming. "The boy drifts into it because there is little else to do, and with a determination on his own part, very often fortified and reinforced by the advice and encouragement of his parents, to get out of it directly he is old enough to leave home and fend for himself." [76] Everyone agreed that, regardless of how many people stood to gain by it, reform of these conditions was long overdue.

When it came to determining the size of the farm population or the ideal type of farm, however, the agrarians spoke mainly for themselves. True to tradition, economists balanced the strategic assets of sea power, a large merchant marine, and overseas customers who could be counted on as wartime allies and suppliers against those of agricultural self-sufficiency.[77] Sir William Beveridge, who fairly represented their views, conceded that some increase in domestic food production might be necessary to offset the loss of foreign investments and the development of competitive foreign industry, but not to the point of protecting "old-fashioned methods" or "a low-paid agricultural population." [78] Neither should it be allowed to increase food prices and depress the general standard of living. On the contrary, the policy should make

76. Agricultural Economics Research Institute, Oxford, *Country Planning*, London, 1944, pp. 1-3 (by permission of Oxford University Press, New York).

77. Cf. Menzies-Kitchin, *op. cit.*, pp. 18-19.

78. Beveridge, William H., *Full Employment in a Free Society*, London, 1944, p. 164.

its primary goal "an adequate standard of nutrition for all classes of the community." [79] British farmers should concentrate on the "protective" foods—milk, dairy products, beef, eggs, poultry, fruit and vegetables—"those foods which can be produced here at less cost in human toil or which cannot readily be transported or stored . . . Britain must have imports. . . ." [80] The objectives were to be achieved, moreover, by full participation in the world economy and the United Nations Food and Agriculture Organization. "Some say that agriculture is necessary for security, others that agriculture is a way of life; more still that the countryside must be preserved, because it breeds healthy and virile manhood. . . . For my part I believe that the test by which agriculture must stand or fall is the job which it is its primary function to perform, that is the production of food economically and as efficiently as possible." [81] So said the British Minister of Agriculture in 1944, and so have thought and voted the British people for a hundred years.

These feelings were not congenial to a wholesale return to the land or a revival of family farming. Britain's international position, her highly industrialized economy, and her overwhelmingly urban society all argued against it. Maximum food production at minimum cost remained the imperative in 1946 as Peel had deemed it to be in 1846. The corollary to this imperative was the most efficient types of farm employing the smallest possible number of people. No doubt this left room for some family farming, in dairying and livestock, for example, but the technical trend toward larger units was unmistakable. It was evident before the war,[82] and the enormous increase in the use of agricultural ma-

79. Menzies-Kitchin, *op. cit.*, p. 63.
80. Beveridge, *op. cit.*, pp. 214-215; Menzies-Kitchin, *op. cit.*, p. 63.
81. Quoted by Menzies-Kitchin, *op. cit.*, pp. 62-63.
82. Cf. Astor and Rowntree, *British Agriculture*, pp. 368-379.

chinery during the war had abetted it. In reporting the results of its wartime survey, the Agricultural Economics Research Institute of Oxford recommended the rearrangement
of farms in the survey area in units ranging from 397 to 654
acres.[83] Part-time allotments were still approved, and small
holdings located here and there, "where small areas, particularly near villages, were found to fit badly into larger
units." [84] But with tractors swarming over the land, the prospect of any substantial increase of family farms was dim;
and with the Labor Party on record in favor of land nation-
alization,[85] the prospect of an expansion of independent ownership—prime qualification of the American family farm—was
even dimmer. As to preserving or expanding the farm population for its influence on the national character and national
political institutions, a Royal Commission that spent two
years investigating every aspect of the problem in 1924 had
probably spoken the last word on the subject:

The conservative instincts, and even the slowness of thinking,
which are supposed to belong to the typical inhabitant of country
districts, are considered to be a good balance, as compared with the
less stable instincts of the town dwellers; and, further, there is a
certain appreciation of the picturesqueness of rural life and character. Because this is a matter of direct appreciation, it is not easy
to give definiteness to these considerations; but many people attach
great importance to them. Now, it is necessary to avoid anything
in the nature of a supercilious or even selfish patronage of rural
life. For the appreciation of rural life which matters is not that of
persons usually resident in towns, who are able to spend convenient
periods in the country in the months when the country is at its
best. The appreciation which matters is that of persons who have
to spend their lives, summer and winter, in scattered villages, cottages and farms. And in all countries, large numbers of these per-

83. *Op. cit.*, pp. 80 ff.
84. *Ibid.*, p. 247.
85. *Our Land*, Labour Party Pamphlet, 1943, pp. 4-5.

sons express that appreciation by the rural exodus. How ideal rural life is, is a matter of opinion, on which they have had something to say.[86]

Thus the thoughts of the post-war planners in 1945 as they made ready to confer upon the rural population the benefits of modern housing, recreation, education, public health, and economic opportunity, of which British democracy had long since availed itself in the cities. Thus the relationship of agrarianism to democracy in the experience of Great Britain.

86. Great Britain, Agricultural Tribunal of Investigation, *Final Report*, 1924, p. 195.

CHAPTER FOUR

The French Contrast

No sooner do we leave England than we perceive that the British attitude toward farming has not spread much farther in the world than the British doctrine of free trade, of which it was a part. With such exceptions as the *Junker* estates of Prussia, Poland, and Hungary, Spanish and Italian *latifundia*, the state farms and collectives of the Soviet Union, and the commercial farms, ranches, and *haciendas* of the Americas and the British dominions, the overwhelming majority of the world's farms are family farms, and most farmers are peasants and family farmers. No other country has permitted its farm population to decline to the British level. In all but eight of them agriculture is still the leading occupation; and those whose industrial development has resembled Britain's have made systematic efforts to protect their farmers against the consequences. One and all have tried to preserve farming—which means, *ipso facto*, family farming—as a preferred way of life and state of society.

This they have done in terms of a variety of political philosophies, a fact which points to the obvious conclusion that family farming does not necessarily produce democracy. The German peasant became an even more privileged character under the Nazi regime than he had been in the Weimar Republic or, for that matter, than the French peasant was in the Third Republic or the family farmer in the American democracy. The individual identity, self-interest, and culture of the Russian peasant has been carefully fostered in the seemingly impersonal organization of the Soviet collective. There is certainly no universal law that equates agrarianism and democracy or family farming and democracy. On the contrary, historical evidence to date seems to indicate that democracy has flourished most in the few countries, with the notable exception of Germany, that have attained a high degree of industrialization and urbanization.

It is true, nevertheless, that all the democratic countries except Great Britain have put a premium on family farming and the agrarian way of life, and none so great a premium as France. France, too, as we have noted of the Physiocrats, has had her advocates of large-scale farming on the British model, and her political leaders have not been blind to the accomplishments of the Russians. But from the beginning of the industrial revolution to the present day, no country has made such a fetish of the small peasant farm—*la petite exploitation familiale,* as it is called—as France.

The best evidence of this is the French landscape. Crossing the Channel in 1787, Arthur Young was amazed at the "sudden and universal" change that confronted him.[1] "The small properties of the peasants are found everywhere, to a degree we have no idea of in England," he noted in his journal; "they are found in every part of the kingdom, even in those provinces where other tenures prevail. . . . I have, more than once, seen division carried to such an excess, that a single fruit tree standing in about 10 perch of ground, has constituted a farm, and the local situation of a family decided by the possession."[2] Young wrote these words before, not after, the French Revolution. They could stand today, unrevised save to emphasize the fact that the patches on the crazy-quilt landscape have grown more numerous and smaller. A British agricultural economist who retraced Young's steps in 1938 heard tales of a single vine plant that

1. Young, Arthur, *Travels in France during the Years 1787, 1788, and 1789.* Maxwell, C., ed., Cambridge, 1929, p. 5.
2. *Ibid.,* p. 295.

constituted a "farm" in one locality and a nut tree shared by three cultivators in another, and put these together with his own observations to conclude that "*parcellement* must be reckoned the major curse of French agriculture." [3]

French agricultural economists agree with him. According to one of their leading representatives, "The 'democratic' division of agricultural property has been carried to excess."

Not only are the total areas cultivated by farmers small, but they are broken up into many small parcels [*émiettées en beaucoup de petites parcelles*]. This is an ancient characteristic of the structure of the French agricultural economy; unfortunately it does not seem to have changed much. One could say that farms are small in every category, not only in the category of very small holdings insufficient to provide a living for a family, but also, in a general way, in the medium, large, or (relatively) very large categories. . . . In France agricultural enterprises are, in general, below the economic and technical optimum in size.[4]

A few statistics will bear out the judgment. France is a nation of 41,000,000 people. Her working population, when last counted, exceeded 21,000,000, of which no less than 7,700,000, or 36 per cent, were employed in agriculture and forestry as compared with 6,800,000, or 31 per cent, in industry. There were at the same time approximately 4,000,000 agricultural holdings of all sizes and varieties, of which 1,000,000 were under 2½ acres, too small to count as farms. Of the 3,000,000 remaining, 1,860,000, or 62 per cent, were under 25 acres, 1,020,000, or 34 per cent, from 25 to 125 acres, and only 120,000, or 4 per cent, over 125 acres. Most remarkable of all, from the British point of view, no less than

3. Yates, *Food Production in Western Europe*, pp. 281-283.
4. Augé-Laribé, M., "Vingt-cinq Ans d'Evolution dans la Structure Agricole Française," *Revue d'Economie Politique*, 1939, Vol. LIII, pp. 125-126. Cf. Salleron, L., *L'Evolution de l'Agriculture Française du Régime Foncier au Régime Corporatif*, Paris, 1937, pp. 9-16.

75 per cent of all holdings, great and small, were owned by those who occupied and cultivated them.[5]

If Britain represents one extreme in the relationship of agrarianism to democracy, France clearly represents the other. She has maintained the largest agricultural population of the three great democracies, larger, in fact, than any country with as long an exposure to the industrial revolution.[6] Though the preference of the French for family farming is typical of most people,[7] the terms in which they have expressed that preference and defended it are uniquely French. *Parcellement* has been carried to a worse and more self-defeating excess in Belgium. Family farming has well-nigh found its universal optimum, both in size and in technical efficiency, in Denmark. But neither of these countries, nor any other, has identified the individual possession and cultivation of the soil with the democratic political philosophy so closely and so literally as France. The agrarian system of France, writes the historian Henri Sée, "has a profoundly original character, which distinguishes it from that of most of the other European countries. This is true to such an extent that even in our own day France has remained a type of rural democracy. In Western

---

5. Twenty per cent were rented by cash tenants and 5 per cent by *métayers* or share tenants. Figures from Yates, *Food Production in Western Europe*, pp. 272-279; International Labour Office, *Year Book of Labour Statistics, 1941*, pp. 5, 11; France, Ministère de l'Economie Nationale, *Annuaire Statistique, 1937*, p. 112.

6. It compares with these as follows:
   (Percentage of working population employed in agriculture)

France	36	Belgium	17
Germany	29	United States	17
Netherlands	21	United Kingdom	6

   League of Nations, Economic Intelligence Service, *Europe's Trade*, Geneva, 1941, p. 50.

7. This is true even of the east European countries where large estate-farming has prevailed. Cf. Warriner, Doreen, *Economics of Peasant Farming*, London, 1939, pp. 2 ff.

Europe it is the only great state in which the equilibrium is not disturbed in favor of industrial development. In this respect the present is closely related to the past." [8]

As we have seen in the case of Great Britain, the present-day characteristics of agricultural production and land ownership derive from the principles of those in power when the state's modern constitution was written and its economy organized. In England, at this critical juncture, the landed aristocracy dominated the government, and the result was the enclosure movement and a general policy of tenancy and large-scale commercial farming. The case of France is strikingly different. There, as Arthur Young discovered in 1787, the peasants occupied, cultivated, and actually possessed the land in small family units, as they had been doing since the days of the medieval manor. Despite the teachings of the Physiocrats, no such wholesale enclosure movement as the British had disturbed this system of agriculture and land tenure. Neither had the industrial revolution, which developed much later, more slowly, and to a much more limited extent in France than it had in England. Consequently, when the French Revolution broke out, the landowning peasant farmers were in a position to influence its course, to sanction by revolutionary law and political philosophy the modes of farming and landowning they already enjoyed by custom. Hence the unusual continuity of the French agricultural system, which even today preserves much of its medieval character.[9]

8. *Economic and Social Conditions in France during the Eighteenth Century*, New York, 1935, p. xvi.

9. In 1852 the medievalist Leopold Delisle declared it had changed so little in eight centuries that a 13th century peasant could visit a 19th century farm "without much astonishment." Clapham, J. H., *The Economic Development of France and Germany*, Cambridge, 1936, p. 6. The most exhaustive study of this subject, from the Roman occupation to the Revolution, is Bloch, Marc, *Les Caractères Originaux de l'Histoire Rurale Française*, Oslo, 1931.

The Revolution settled what had been, and would continue to be, the outstanding social question in Europe from 1500 to 1850, the question of the peasants. Napoleon accepted its results, and so, one after the other, did most of France's neighbors. Her disposition of the question "stood throughout the nineteenth century," says Clapham, "and stands today. . . . From her revolutionary land settlement, through peasant emancipation in Prussia, to the emancipation of the Russian serfs, and even to the modern land legislation for Ireland, there is a continuous historic chain." [10] The chain reaches even farther, as we shall see—to the Bankhead-Jones Farm Tenancy Act, the Farm Security Administration, and the agrarian policy of the New Deal.

It is difficult for us, to whom the word "revolution" signifies the expropriation and collectivizing of the peasants, to realize that the French Revolution meant exactly the opposite. When it began, France was a nation of 24,000,000 people, 20,000,000 of whom were peasants. The conditions in which these peasants lived and worked were radically different from those in England.[11] In the first place they were by far the most important group of landowners, both in number and in extent of property. They constituted 90 per

10. Clapham, *Economic Development of France and Germany*, pp. 1-2.

11. The authorities for this account are: Sée, Henri, *Economic and Social Conditions in France during the Eighteenth Century*, New York, 1936, *passim*; Gershoy, Leo, *The French Revolution and Napoleon*, New York, 1933, Ch. II; Lefèbvre, G., "Les Recherches Relatives à la Répartition de la Propriété et de l'Exploitation Foncières à la Fin de l'Ancien Régime," *Revue d'Histoire Moderne*, 1928, Vol. III, pp. 103-130; "La Place de la Révolution dans l'Histoire Agraire de la France," *Annales d'Histoire Economique et Sociale*, 1929, Vol. I, pp. 506-519; and "La Révolution Française et les Paysans," *Cahiers de la Révolution Française*, 1934, Vol. I, pp. 7-49; Bloch, Marc, *Les Caractères Originaux de l'Histoire Rurale Française*, esp. Chs. IV-VI.

cent of all French landowners and owned 40 per cent of the land, reducing to numerical insignificance the 250,000 nobles and 130,000 clergy who, together, owned about 30 per cent, and the more prosperous bourgeois landowners with 15 per cent.[12] Four million, or between 70 and 80 per cent of all adult male peasants, were landowners, and most of the remainder were tenant farmers on the estates of nobles and clergy. Their ranks were completed by a landless agricultural proletariat, by no means as large or as important as the British, and about a million serfs.

In the second place, agricultural production was carried on—planned, managed, and executed—almost entirely by these peasants in small individual units. Large-scale commercial farms of the British type were virtually non-existent, and even the fifty-acre farms of the more prosperous peasants (*laboureurs*) were few and far between. Much of the land owned by the nobles and clergy consisted of uncultivated forests, moors, and meadows in which the peasants enjoyed common rights of wood-cutting and pasture; and almost all of their cultivated land was leased to peasants in small parcels. As Tocqueville said of them, the British aristocracy had exchanged privilege for political power, the French, political power for privilege.[13] The British aristocracy was enclosing the land and actively farming it; the French preferred to live on the feudal dues and rents they collected from the peasants and leave the actual work of farming entirely in their hands. The Physiocrats and their disciples, most of whom were wealthy bourgeois and magistrates, constituted a minority and an exception to this rule. By 1789 the division of labor, with respect to agriculture, between the

12. These are rough national averages based on the estimates of Sée and Lefèbvre.
13. Hammond, J., *Village Labourer*, p. 1; Bloch, *Les Caractères Originaux de l'Histoire Rurale Française*, pp. 139 ff.

peasants and the privileged classes had become fixed in custom and, in so far as the latter were concerned, in economic necessity.

This was true not only of the nobles who leased their estates in small holdings to cash tenants (*fermiers*) or sharecroppers (*métayers*), but also, and more particularly, of those who lived on feudal dues from the land owned by the peasants. The peasants owned this land in the sense that they occupied and cultivated it and could buy, sell, lease, bequeath, or inherit it; but they did not own it outright, in the modern alodial sense. Their title was feudal: subject, that is, to the payment to the nobles of certain dues, such as quitrents, and to the enjoyment upon it by the nobles of certain rights and privileges, such as local justice, fishing, hunting, and fowling. To all practical intents and purposes the peasants were its true owners. The nobles owned it as concessionaires to its revenues and privileges. These, together with the multiplicity of taxes [14] from which they and the clergy were for the most part exempt, bore down heavily upon the peasants and were the first objective of their revolutionary uprisings.

The standard of living of most of the peasants was extremely low. The holdings of the vast majority of landowners were too small to provide their families a living, forcing them to eke out their existence as sharecroppers or casual laborers. Large numbers of the latter lived in mud huts, hardly bigger or cleaner than kennels, and managed to keep themselves alive by working in the fields, scavenging, and begging. Often the only thing that stood between them and starvation was the right to cut wood and pasture a few livestock on the local commons and fallow fields. Hunger

---

14. Such as the *taille* (land or property), *capitation* (poll tax), *vingtième* (income), *gabelle* (salt), *corvée* (personal service), *aides* (excise), *douanes* (customs), tithe (church), etc.

was chronic among them and, in bad years (as in 1789), starvation widespread.

The cause of their predicament lay partly in the corruption of the *ancien régime* and the utter inefficiency of its mercantilist economy. It was even more fundamentally rooted in the soil. Too many people were trying to make a living out of agriculture. France was one of the most densely populated countries in Europe. Her birth rate was rising. The agricultural population had already exhausted the supply of land and outstripped the existing means of production. On top of all this it was called upon to bear most of the costs of government and the expenses of nobles and clergy. The land was being asked to produce more wealth than it was possibly capable of producing. It could not employ all who were living on it; it could not even feed them. Yet the agrarian fundamentalism of the French, the love of the soil and the faith in its productive powers, was unshaken.

There were a few individuals who believed that the only remedy for these conditions was the British—wholesale enclosure, commercial farming, industrialization—and in the decade preceding the Revolution, Louis XVI made a belated attempt to try it out. He issued decrees in several provinces permitting the nobles to incorporate one-third of the commons within their estates. He concluded a commercial treaty with England (1786), lifted the tariff on domestic commerce in grain (1787), and in various other ways, such as reclaiming uncultivated meadows and promoting local industries, tried to increase agricultural production and provide employment for the excess agricultural population. Every one of these reforms was frustrated by the opposition of the peasants or the nobles, or both. Enclosing the commons, of which relatively few remained, deprived many landless peasants of their sole source of fuel and food. Commercial farming required the consolidation (*remembrement*) of small parcels in larger and more efficient units. To the peasants this meant wholesale expropriation, to the nobles, the loss of income from feudal dues, to the king, a dangerous increase in the rural proletariat. The treaty with England and domestic free trade in grain roused the peasants' fear that local storehouses would be emptied for distant markets. The peasants were divided against themselves: the poor wanted to maintain the commons, the well-to-do to enclose them. Even the Physiocrats, who believed in commercial farming and free trade, opposed industrialism. The royal reforms were lost in the chaos.[15]

The real desires of the French people in 1789 and the true relationship of agrarianism and democracy in France were revealed in the laws affecting agricultural property enacted during the Revolution, particularly the constitutional definitions of the property right, the laws abolishing feudalism, the laws governing the confiscation and sale of the estates of the clergy and *émigré* nobility, and the laws concerning inheritance. In one sense these laws were practical applications of the natural rights philosophy inherited from Locke by the French *philosophes* and passed on by them, with the added prestige of the American example, to the leaders of the Revolution. In a more concrete sense they were a rationalization of the existing system of agriculture, stripped of its feudal privileges. They made a strange combination of the old and the new, the conservative and the radical, the ancient ways and the new ideas.

The first constitutional definition of the property right occurred in the Declaration of the Rights of Man and of the Citizen, adopted by the Constituent Assembly on August 27,

15. See esp. Lefèbvre, "La Place de la Révolution," *loc. cit.*, and Bloch, *op. cit.*, pp. 223-239, and "La Lutte pour l'Individualisme Agraire dans la France du XVIIIe Siècle," *Annales d'Histoire Economique et Sociale*, 1930, Vol. II, pp. 329-381, 511-551.

1789, and subsequently incorporated in the Constitution of 1791. The philosophy of the Declaration resembled nothing more closely than that of the Virginia Bill of Rights, a copy of which Jefferson had furnished Lafayette, at the latter's request when the Declaration was being written.[16] It was the latest expression of the laissez-faire individualism that was the revolutionary testament of the time. "The aim of every political association," it declared, "is the preservation of the natural and imprescriptible rights of man," and these were enumerated as "Liberty, property, security, and resistance to oppression." [17] Liberty consisted of "the power to do anything that does not injure others," and the state was confined to the civil role of forbidding "only such actions as are injurious to society."

A year and a half later (April 24, 1793), Robespierre submitted a new Declaration of Rights to the National Convention, which had succeeded the Constituent Assembly. In this document, while property was still a "natural . . . sacred and inalienable" right, its use and possession were somewhat restricted. A citizen could do as he wished with his property, "which the law guarantees him," provided he did not "prejudice the security, nor the liberty, nor the existence, nor the property of our fellow creatures." [18] This sounds more like the self-limiting property concepts of Locke and Jefferson: liberty tempered by equality. But in the Constitution of the Year I (1793),[19] the property right was unqualified. The Constitution of the Year III, which went into effect October 26, 1795, proclaimed private property as both a right and a

16. Chinard, *Thomas Jefferson*, pp. 232 ff.
17. For text see Anderson, Frank M., ed., *The Constitutions and Other Select Documents Illustrative of the History of France, 1789-1907*, Minneapolis, 1908, pp. 59 ff.
18. *Ibid.*, pp. 160-164.
19. Accepted by the people and the Convention, June 23, 1793, but never put into effect. *Ibid.*, pp. 171-184.

duty. As a right it was one with liberty, security, and equality, "the right to enjoy and dispose of one's goods, and income, and the fruit of one's labor and industry." As a duty: "It is upon the maintenance of property that the cultivation of the land, all the productions, all means of labor, and the whole social order rest." [20] Finally the *Code Napoléon,* promulgated February 6, 1804, and the civil code of France until this day:

Art. 544. Ownership is the right to enjoy and dispose of things in the most absolute manner, provided they are not used in a way prohibited by law or regulations.

Art. 545. No one can be compelled to give up his property, unless it is for public use and for a proper indemnity previously given.

Art. 546. The ownership of personal or real property gives the right to everything it produces and to what is added to it, by way of accession either naturally or artificially. [21]

Thus the French people laid down the constitutional principles of private property in the Revolution, and thus they continued to maintain them throughout their history. The Constitutional Charter of 1814 called property "inviolable," as did the Constitution of 1830. [22] The Constitution of 1848 adopted for its basis "the family, labor, property, and public order," acknowledged the duty of the state to protect the citizen in each, and again declared all property "inviolable." [23] Louis Napoleon's Constitution of 1852 reaffirmed the right, in a clause guaranteeing "the great principles of 1789 . . . which are the basis of the public law of the French." [24] The Constitution of the Third Republic (1875) left it unchanged. And the Constitution of the Fourth Republic, adopted Oc-

20. *Ibid.,* pp. 212 ff.
21. Cachard, H., ed., *The French Civil Code,* Paris, 1930, p. 174.
22. Anderson, *op. cit.,* pp. 459 ff., 507 ff.
23. *Ibid.,* pp. 523-535 ff.
24. *Ibid.,* p. 544.

tober 13, 1946, "solemnly reaffirms the rights and liberties of man and of the citizen consecrated by the Declaration of Rights of 1789 and the fundamental principles recognized by the laws of the Republic."[25] The belief in private property has been the common denominator of all French parties and political philosophies, the center of gravity of French democracy.

Except in a literal, constitutional sense, this belief did not suddenly dawn on the country in 1789. It had gathered strength steadily since Roman times, as evidenced in the infinite division and subdivision (*parcellement*) of the agricultural land. The one purpose all classes had in common was to maintain or acquire private property in land. It is true, as French historians[26] have emphasized, that the possession of property tended to divide those who had it from those who had not, that the majority of poor peasants clung to the rights of common pasture and forest, and that those rights constituted limitations upon the right of private property. Yet the same authorities have admitted that the humblest peasant wanted nothing so much as to buy or rent a little land.[27] Of this prevailing sentiment the demands of the peasants and the laws passed to satisfy them were proof. To them the Revolution was the means to the end of preserving the existing agricultural system with themselves in possession of it.

Their first aim, then, was to secure full legal title to the land whose fruits they were forced to share with the nobles and clergy, to translate their feudal title into outright fee-

25. Text from *France*, Oct. 4, 1946, pp. 11-12. The Constitution, originally providing for a unicameral legislature, was rejected by the people (May 5, 1946) in favor of the more conservative Constitution adopted October 13, 1946.
26. E.g., Lefèbvre, "La Révolution Française et les Paysans," *loc. cit.*, and Bloch, "La Lutte pour l'Individualisme," *loc. cit.*
27. As Lefèbvre says, "ne fût-ce qu'un courtil et une misérable chaumière." "La Place de la Révolution," *loc. cit.*, p. 510.

simple ownership. This they accomplished partially on August 4, 1789, and completely on July 17, 1793. On the first of these occasions the Constituent Assembly, moved to action as much by peasant revolts in the provinces as by the storming of the Bastille, abolished outright serfdom, the tithe, tax-exemptions, and the particularly obnoxious hunting and fishing privileges, in short, all "rights and dues . . . originating in or representing real or personal serfdom, or personal servitude." [28] Between these personal obligations and privileges and the feudal dues and rents originating in the land itself, however, the Assembly drew a significant distinction. It construed the latter as private property, declared them redeemable, and ruled that they should continue to be collected "until indemnification takes place." So it happened that the peasants, rejoicing in the opening sentence of the decree, "The National Assembly completely abolishes the feudal regime," were dismayed to find the nobles showing up with their feudal lawyers to make the usual collections. Against this practice and its beneficiaries they presented a united front, resisting so stubbornly that the Constituent Assembly found compromise impossible and the National Convention finally abolished all feudal dues without exception or indemnification.[29] The long delay speaks eloquently of the restraint with which the Revolutionary governments laid hands on even this most unpopular form of private property.[30]

The second great demand of the peasants was for land. They saw the abstract principle of private property in the

28. Anderson, *op. cit.*, pp. 11 ff.
29. For text of the decree of July 17, 1793, see Duvergier, J. B., ed., *Collection Complète des Lois, Décrets, Ordonnances, Réglemens, Avis du Conseil-d'Etat*, Paris, 1834, Vol. VI, pp. 19-24.
30. Lefèbvre goes so far as to suggest that even some bourgeois and more prosperous peasant landowners, who stood to gain by the reform, opposed it lest it undermine the principle of private property," cf. his "La Place de la Révolution," *loc. cit.*, p. 507.

concrete form of agricultural property, "were it only a tiny garden and a miserable thatched hut." When the Constituent Assembly confiscated the lands of the clergy (November 2, 1789), it was deluged with peasant *cahiers* urging that the lands be distributed among them.[31] The *cahiers* originated with large numbers of landless peasants as well as owners and tenants of parcels too small to live on. But the Assembly had confiscated the ecclesiastical land for financial rather than for charitable reasons. The government needed it as collateral for its paper *assignats*. To maintain their value (and its own solvency) it was obliged to realize as much as it possibly could from the land by selling it at auction. As the Revolution progressed and the country became involved in wars with its counterrevolutionary neighbors, its financial difficulties increased, forcing the National Convention to follow the example of the Assembly. By decrees of 1792 and 1793, the lands of *émigré* nobles, political suspects, colleges, and charitable institutions were added to those already confiscated and their sale at auction continued.

All this while the peasants maintained constant pressure on the changing governments to distribute the confiscated land. They wanted it free, or on easy terms of purchase or lease, in small parcels. Nor did they confine their attention to the *biens nationaux:* they demanded the subdivision of the larger bourgeois and peasant farms. The theme common to all their memorials was the superiority of small farms over large, and the urgent necessity of increasing the number of the former

31. Text of decree, Anderson, *op. cit.*, p. 15. For details of the confiscation and sale of the national lands (*biens nationaux*) see esp. Lefèbvre, "Les Recherches Relatives à la Vente des Biens Nationaux," *Revue d'Histoire Moderne*, 1928, Vol. III, pp. 188-219; "La Révolution Française et les Paysans," *loc. cit.*; and *Questions Agraires aux Temps de la Terreur*, Strasbourg, 1932; Sée, Henri, *Esquisse d'une Histoire Economique et Sociale de la France*, Paris, 1929, pp. 377-379, 382 ff.

by reducing the size of the latter.[32] A petition from the municipality of Rozet-les-Menils dated June 22, 1794, for example, contended that a farm of 400 *arpents*,[33] divided into twenty farms of 20 *arpents* each, would support six times as many cattle. Equal division of the land would not cause the collapse of the social order. A farm of 300 *arpents* was the largest that should belong to any one man. A small farm, well tended, with a definite horizon (*un horizon borné, mais clair*), that was what happiness and reason demanded. A maximum of 300 *arpents* was equitable and sufficient. If the objection be raised that large farms were necessary to provide the experience essential to progress, let the government reserve a portion of the *émigré* lands for that purpose.[34] The Department of the Aisne suggested a maximum of 240 *arpents*, the Société Populaire et Régenérée d'Hargicourt, one of 100 *arpents*, the Société Populaire de Boulay, 100 *arpents*, and so on, the amount varying inversely with the density of the local population.[35]

There was almost no political philosophy in these petitions: they were practical and moralistic. Their authors were poor and hungry. They wanted land. The way to obtain land was to subdivide the large farms and the *biens nationaux*. This would be good for the country as well as for the peasants because small-scale farming (*la petite culture*) was superior to large-scale (*la grande culture*). It was more productive, and it was more just.

Since it matters very much to the public welfare that the farmer remain in his primitive situation, from which he never should have

32. See the original documents from the National Archives published under the auspices of the Ministry of Public Instruction by Lefèbvre in *Questions Agraires*, pp. 136-236.
33. An *arpent* was about 1½ acres.
34. Text from Lefèbvre, *Questions Agraires*, pp. 139-140.
35. *Ibid.*, pp. 141 ff.

departed—he who, by his condition, is responsible to his fellows as
both trustee and steward [*le dépositeur et l'économe*] for the advantages that nature puts in his hands for their subsistence; representative citizens, you will come to this great measure, which has
today become so necessary to execute for the public tranquillity:
order the reduction of the great farms, so that each farmer shall
be prohibited from exploiting a greater quantity of cultivated land
than that which would employ two, or at most three, ploughs.[36]

This petition from Baudier et Lasne (February 21, 1795)
came as near to political philosophy as any of them.

Not until its hand was forced by counterrevolution at home
as well as by military invasion from abroad did the government acquiesce in these demands. Impelled by the Girondist
uprising in the spring of 1793 to rally the poor peasants to
their support, the Robespierrists made a few concessions. By
decrees of June 3 and 10, they provided for the sale of *biens
nationaux* on the installment plan, thus admitting to their
purchase many peasants hitherto excluded by lack of capital,
and they withdrew from auction a portion of the *biens* to be
subdivided and sold directly to heads of families owning less
than 1 *arpent*, in amounts not to exceed 1 *arpent*, at a nominal
price payable in ten equal installments.[37] The weakening of
the *assignat* soon caused them to regret the loss of revenue
entailed in the latter practice, however, and by a decree of
September 13, they abandoned it in favor of an outright cash
relief payment of 500 livres per family. These measures put
more land into circulation but fell a long way short of satis-
fying the poor peasants. They did not stop the sale of land
at auction. They hardly put a dent in the excess agricultural
population. One *arpent* was not nearly enough to provide a
man a living; and when the books were finally balanced, it
was found that more of the land had gone to augment the

36. *Ibid.*, p. 208.
37. *Ibid.*, p. 31.

holdings of the well-to-do than to eke out the possessions of the small-holders or relieve the indigent.[38] The practical needs of the treasury and the deep-rooted belief in private property and free enterprise had prevailed over the cautious equalitarianism of the most radical of revolutionary governments.[39]

In a larger sense the old agrarian system of France had prevailed over the Revolution. With feudalism abolished, equality before the law established, and the aristocracy eliminated as a unifying factor, rural society receded, as it were, into its component parts and resumed its ancient ways. The large majority of the peasants who were property-owners went right on cultivating and, if possible, expanding their holdings exactly as they had done for generations, with little change in technique or outlook. The minority who did not own land continued on the one hand to resist the enclosure of commons and on the other to strive by one means or another to become property-owners themselves. They did not wish to burn the bridge that separated them from the landowners, but to cross it. Few thought in economic terms of the fundamental problem in whose toils all were caught, regardless of social position: the steadily increasing overpopulation of a steadily decreasing supply of agricultural land.

There is no better proof of their intentions than the laws of inheritance, one more venerable tradition that was merely

38. This conclusion, in which Sée, Lefèbvre, Bloch and other authorities on the subject concur, is most fully documented by Lefèbvre in "Les Recherches Relatives à la Vente des Biens Nationaux," *loc. cit.*, and expanded by him in all of his works cited above.

39. Augé-Laribé emphasizes the practical nature of the legislation in question which he says "n'est pas le résultat de convictions théoriques" but was motivated "seulement par des nécessités politiques et financières." *Grande ou Petite Propriété*, Montpellier, 1902, p. 42.

codified by the Revolution. In Britain, laws of primogeniture and entail had enabled the landed aristocracy to preserve its inherited estates intact since medieval times, and though the practice declined in the latter half of the nineteenth century, the laws themselves were not abolished until 1925.[40] In France, particularly among the peasants, exactly the opposite practice had prevailed, namely that of equal inheritance. Translating this custom into law, the Assembly abolished primogeniture, and in a sweeping series of property laws enacted January 6-10, 1794, the Convention made the equal division of property among heirs compulsory.[41] This law was incorporated in the *Code Napoléon* in 1803 and stands today as Article 745 of the Civil Code of France.[42] As a custom, Arthur Young had written of it:

> Forty or fifty acres in property are not incapable of good husbandry; but when divided, twenty acres *must* be ill cultivated; again divided, they become farms of ten acres, of five, of two, and even one; and I have seen some of half, and even a quarter of a rood, with a family as much attached to it, as if it were a hundred acres. The population flowing from this division is, in some cases, great, but it is the multiplication of wretchedness. Couples marry and procreate on the *idea*, not the *reality*, of a maintenance; they increase beyond the demand of towns and manufactures, and the consequence is, distress, and numbers dying of diseases, arising from insufficient nourishment. Hence, therefore, small properties, much divided, prove the greatest source of misery that can be conceived; and this has operated to such an extent and degree in France, that a law undoubtedly ought to be passed, to render all division, below a certain number of arpents, illegal.[43]

40. Primogeniture was made permissive by the Law of Property Act of 1925. Cf. Cheshire, G. C., *The Modern Law of Real Property*, 5th ed., London, 1944, pp. 348 ff.
41. The laws were retroactive to 1789. For text and explanatory notes see Duvergier, *Lois*, Vol. VI, pp. 373-384, esp. arts. 62-90.
42. Cachard, *French Civil Code*, p. 223.
43. *Travels in France*, pp. 299-300.

Democracy to the French peasants meant equal opportunity to share the dwindling supply of agricultural land and to persist in their way of living, even at the cost of "the multiplication of wretchedness."

By making the practice of equal inheritance part of its law and political theory, the Revolution gave it a practically unbreakable lease on life. For as we shall see, when French converts to Arthur Young's point of view began to gain headway in the government, they encountered Article 745 of the Civil Code as a stone wall, with the peasants solidly behind it. Their resistance was so strong to any and all attempts at consolidating the myriad parcels in larger and more economical holdings that one of the policy's most sympathetic critics accorded it slight chance of success. "In this respect," he wrote in 1934, "our capitalist evolution has been very slow and remained very imperfect; it has not destroyed the autonomy of the small rural producer who is the foundation of our political democracy. . . . It is because France has had a peasant revolution. It is also because the Revolution created with us, in politics, an equalitarian and democratic tradition." [44]

The Revolution was not a complete triumph for the peasants, especially the poor peasants. It was rather a triumph for laissez-faire government and free enterprise, in which large-scale bourgeois and peasant farmers profited more conspicuously than family farmers and small-holders. Yet the domain of the latter was extended commensurately with their legal security and political prestige. If, as the eminent French historian Marc Bloch suggests, the Revolution had broken out three hundred years earlier, all of the land might have been divided among small-holders; for in those days no one stood

44. Lefèbvre, "La Révolution Française et les Paysans," *loc. cit.*, p. 41.

between the nobles, who would have been liquidated, and their serfs and tenants—"small occupiers"—who would have taken the land.[45] In the three centuries intervening, the holdings of large landowners had grown until they almost equaled the infinitely more numerous family farms and small holdings in extent of acreage. During the Revolution the number of small independent landowners increased in certain provinces by as much as 35 per cent.[46] The increase can be attributed partly to the sale of *biens nationaux,* partly to the voluntary sales of large landowners, forced by hard times to convert some of their holdings into cash, but in greatest measure, to the operation of the law of equal inheritance in combination with a rise in the total population from 24,000,000 in 1789 to 29,000,000 in 1805.[47] In this respect, as in so many others, the Revolution put the seal of constitutional finality on trends that had been in motion since the Middle Ages, trends that included the fundamentals of modern French agrarianism and French democracy. But it left the landless peasants dissatisfied, and it did not solve the agricultural problem. By multiplying the number of smallholders, it retarded not only the industrial revolution but also the technical development of agriculture itself. "Thus," says Bloch, "the past commands the present. . . ."[48]

The revolutionary pattern of French agriculture and agrarian life has remained virtually impervious to time and political change. The one-tenth of the land still in commons in 1815—mostly woods and upland pastures in the mountainous areas—was gradually enclosed. The practice of common pasture on fallow fields slowly declined, though it never

45. Bloch, *Les Caractères Originaux,* p. 154.
46. See figures in Lefèbvre, "Les Recherches Relatives à la Vente des Biens Nationaux," *loc. cit.,* p. 217.
47. *Annuaire Statistique, 1937,* "Résumé Rétrospectif," p. 11.
48. Bloch, *Les Caractères Originaux,* p. 250.

wholly disappeared.[49] No doubt its survival was evidence of the primitive communalism that had long been present in French rural life. But the predominant trait of the millions of small farmers was individualism. Even their exercise of common rights was individualistic. There was not one good cultivator, a contemporary French observer reported in 1812, "who would not vote for the abolition of a right, which is as injurious to the rotation of crops and the abolition of fallows as to the prosperity of sheep rearing. . . . Often two and even three shepherds arrive almost at the same moment in a field recently reaped to feed their flocks. Each hustles his sheep with his dogs to get there first; and, in the end, the two latest arrived have tired their flocks to no purpose, for they have to go elsewhere." [50] The typical peasant was jealous of his newly won property rights and resented interference, whether from his neighbors and their livestock or from the government.

The one serious challenge to the system merely served to prove its strength. This occurred in the reign of the Restoration monarch Charles X. Charles's predecessor, Louis XVIII, had followed Napoleon's example and accepted the agrarian and property laws of the Revolution. Charles and his supporters determined to revise them, in particular to abolish the law of equal inheritance and restore the right of primogeniture and entail. They wished to reconstitute an hereditary landed aristocracy as the surest foundation for the monarchy. Immediately they encountered opposition. The émigrés had been trooping back to France and recouping their losses, the government had just voted them a billion-

49. Clapham, *Economic Development of France and Germany*, pp. 12 ff.; Bloch, "La Lutte pour l'Individualisme," *loc. cit.*, pp. 543-551.
50. *La Statistique Agricole de 1814*, quoted by Clapham, *Economic Development of France and Germany*, p. 13.

franc indemnity for their confiscated estates, and the public's fears were aroused that the restoration of primogeniture fitted into a reactionary program to bring back the *ancien régime*.[51]

The debate on the proposed law lasted three months (March 11 to May 11, 1826) and was the *cause célèbre* of the year. The long-winded orations of peers, ministers, and deputies, filling hundreds of pages in the *Archives Parlementaires*, convey little of the contemporary excitement it evoked. This was the more remarkable in view of the mildness of the law. It applied only to the disposable portion of an estate, which was limited by Article 913[52] of the Civil Code to the same fraction as that of each child—½ if there was one child, ⅓ if there were two, and so on. It was permissive, not obligatory, restricted in application to estates paying a minimum land tax of 300 francs, and provided for entailment to the eldest son only in case no other disposition of the property had been made by testament.[53] Even so it was hotly contested. For every peer who argued that it would strengthen the family, which both sides agreed was the cornerstone of French society, another argued that it would weaken it. The contention that *parcellement* was being carried to a pernicious extreme and could only be corrected by settling estates on single heirs and keeping them intact by entail was met by the assertion that equal inheritance was the best means of spreading property, and with it responsibility, among the greatest number of people. The one aim all mem-

---

51. Lavisse, Ernest, ed., *Histoire de France contemporaine*, Paris, 1920-22, Vol. IV, pp. 235-243; Augé-Laribé, M., *Grande ou Petite Propriété*, pp. 53-68; Viel-Castel, Louis de, *Histoire de la Restauration*, Paris, 1873, Vol. XV, pp. 212-315; *Archives Parlementaires*, 2nd series (1800-1860), Vols. XLVI, XLVII, specific passages cited below.

52. Cachard, *op. cit.*, p. 264.

53. For the various versions of the law as it passed through the Chamber of Peers, see *Archives Parlementaires*, Vol. XLVI, esp. p. 265.

bers of the upper house seem to have had in common was to keep French society conservative. The issue was whether *grande propriété*, ensured by primogeniture and entail, or *petite propriété*, ensured by equal inheritance, was the better means to this end.

The advocates of small farms and equal inheritance won. They whittled the law down to a single article merely permitting temporary entailment of the disposable fraction of an estate—"débris from the shipwreck of the right of primogeniture," one deputy called it [54]—and in this form sent it to the Deputies. Their action touched off several days of popular celebrations: illuminations, *feux de joie*, firecrackers, and parades and demonstrations. Crowds gathered outside the Chamber of Peers to cheer the members as they emerged, and the press depicted parents raising their hands toward heaven in gratitude for the salvation of peace and justice in the home. An antisocial, anti-French law, "which the minister of privilege and prejudice, of routine and superstition had cast in the midst of a stupefied nation," had been rejected.[55]

In the view of the Duc de Broglie, one of the outstanding opponents of primogeniture, small farms were technically inferior to large, but for political and social reasons were better suited to France. As he saw it, the real issue of the debate was neither laws of inheritance nor methods of farming. The proposed law was "not a law but a declaration of principles, a manifesto against the actual state of Society." The right of primogeniture was the foundation of inequality;

54. Augé-Laribé, *Grande ou Petite Propriété*, p. 64. As received and passed by the Chamber of Deputies, the law provided that gifts *inter vivos* or by will could be made in whole or in part with the charge that they be returned by the donee to one or more of his children, born or to be born, up to the second degree inclusive. For text see *Archives Parlementaires*, Vols. XLVII, LXXVIII.

55. Viel-Castel, *op. cit.*, pp. 291 ff.

it was "privilege pure, absolute, without disguise or compensation . . . a positive law which is not demanded by any natural law." Legal inequality among the sons of a family meant legal inequality between the different branches of a family, "between the diverse families of which the nation is composed," between different types of occupation and property. This amounted to "a social and political revolution, a revolution against the Revolution." De Broglie admitted that primogeniture existed in England, in a form "a hundred times more harsh and unjust" than the one under discussion. There, all of the landed property went to the eldest son, everything, without exception. In England, class distinctions were observed "with a punctilious and pedantic exactitude," and the government was dominated by a few great families, a "vast corporation of gentlemen who, in the names of justices of the peace, grand juries, do all, decide all, dispose of all." But the English aristocracy was a unique and "imposing phenomenon in the world and in history." It had identified itself with the interests of the people. It had "run the same risks, defended the same cause, fought the same fight." But a British aristocracy could never be created in France by a law so abhorrent to the people as primogeniture, a law which they opposed "less as a bad law than as an evil thought." [56]

In the Chamber of Deputies the issue was defined in much the same terms. Behind the "fragment of a mutilated law" lay a bad principle, an entering wedge for more dangerous things to come. In its original text the law had legalized inequality, and with it all that was vicious in man's moral nature. Giving the lion's share to the eldest son would increase his vanity in proportion with his brothers' servility. It was subversive of the *Code civil*—"last guarantee of the rights of Frenchmen," the first shot fired against the revo-

56. *Archives Parlementaires*, Vol. XLVI, pp. 610-624.

lutionary institutions to the creation of which the country
had devoted thirty years of storm and struggle.

The man who has nothing to lose is a menace to society, I do
not deny it; but he who can lose much without being ruined is no
less dangerous. One risks what he does not have: it matters little
to him; the other risks a part of what he has, it matters little to
him either, for he hopes to gain a great deal or save the rest. The
only man who is attached to the established order is he who possessing only limited means cannot risk anything without risking
everything. Study history. Men without property are the instruments of factions; but the leaders of the factions have always been
grands propriétaires.[57]

With this classic statement of the *petit bourgeois* ideal, the
leftist leader Benjamin Constant cast his ballot against the
mutilated law. It was passed over his opposition and promulgated May 17, 1826, only to prove ineffectual and to be
abrogated in 1849.[58]

The speeches of these liberal peers and deputies implied
no such deliberate choice between agriculture and industry
as the British made with the repeal of the Corn Laws twenty
years later. They barely came to grips with the economic
aspects of the question. They are more interesting for the
popular excitement they stirred up than for their content.
The excitement showed the strength of the tradition of
family farming and landowning, a tradition to which national politics gravitated as filings to a magnet.

In France as elsewhere this tradition was molded into a
distinct concept of life and society by the pressure of the industrial revolution. The pressure was not applied suddenly,
as in England, but gradually, and never with such force.
The revolution did not really begin in France until 1830 and
did not gain full momentum until after 1850. Of the many

57. *Archives Parlementaires,* Vol. XLVII, pp. 681-687.
58. Augé-Laribé, *Grande ou Petite Propriété,* p. 68.

factors that combined to retard its progress and limit its ultimate dimensions, two of the most important were lack of coal and political instability. Coal is the foundation of modern industry, and of this vital resource France is capable of producing barely one-fifth as much as Britain or Germany, or one-eighth as much as the United States.[59] Again, France's chronic revolutions and changes of political regime hampered the development of long-range economic policies and seriously disrupted her economic life. Thus, although the industrial revolution was attended by the same phenomena (such as a rural exodus, the rise of cities, mechanization, and the concentration of productive resources in fewer and larger units) as attended it everywhere, it never made such a complete conquest as it did in Britain, Germany, or the United States. While the total British population increased from 11,000,000 in 1801 to 45,000,000 in 1931, the French increased only from 27,500,000 to 41,000,000; and although the proportion of the population employed in agriculture declined as that in industry increased, it sank no lower than 36 per cent.[60] By count of numbers employed, and especially by comparison with the other three powers, France remained primarily an agricultural country.

59. The maximum amount produced by each of the four in any year was France, 68,500,000 (1929), United Kingdom, 345,000,000 (1937), Germany, 368,000,000 (1937), U.S.A., 615,000,000 (1918) metric tons. *Annuaire Statistique*, 1937, pp. 335-337. The coal reserves of the four nations have been estimated as follows (in 1,000 million metric tons): France, 17; Germany, 181; Britain, 190; U.S.A., 2,736. H. Kranold, *International Distribution of Raw Materials*, New York, 1937, pp. 218-219.

60. Figures from Clapham, *Economic History of Modern Britain*, Vol. I, p. 53; *Annuaire Statistique*, 1937. Cf. pp. 48-50 above. Main trends of French economic history in the nineteenth century from Clapham, *Econ. Development of France and Germany*, esp. Chs. III, VIII, X; Sée, Henri, *Esquisse d'une Histoire Economique et Sociale de la France*, pp. 422-513; Viallate, A., *L'Activité Economique en France*, Paris, 1937, *passim*.

Second in importance only to the lack of coal and unstable politics as a factor in this development was the attachment of the French to farming as a way of life and to family farming and equal inheritance as basic social institutions. The more this attachment was strained, the stronger it seemed to grow; the greater the advance of industry and commerce, the more tenaciously the small farmer clung to his farm and the more his life was idealized in contrast with that of the clerk or factory hand. The economist Sismondi expressed the feelings of most of his countrymen in a typical tribute to family farming in 1887:

Wherever peasant proprietors are found, one recognizes also that freedom, that security, that confidence in the future, that independence, which assures at the same time happiness and virtue. The peasant who with the assistance of his children performs all the work on his small heritage, who neither pays rent to anyone above him nor wages to anyone below, who regulates his production by his consumption, who eats his own wheat, drinks his own wine, clothes himself with his own hemp and wool, troubles himself little to know the price of the market; for he has little to sell and little to buy, and he is never ruined by commercial revolutions. Far from fearing the future, he sees it grow beautiful in his trust [s'embellir dans son espérance]; for he puts to profit for his children, for centuries to come, every instant that does not require his seasonal labor. It takes only a few moments of work to put into the ground the seed that in a hundred years will be a great tree, to dig the ditch that will drain his field forever, to build the conduit that will bring him a supply of fresh water, to improve by his cares, often repeated but salvaged from lost moments, every kind of animal and vegetable with which he surrounds himself. His little patrimony is a true savings bank, always ready to receive all his small profits, to use all his moments of leisure. The constantly active power of nature makes them fruitful and returns them a hundred-fold.[61]

61. Quoted by Augé-Laribé, *Grande ou Petite Prop.*, pp. 69-70, from *Etudes sur l'Economie Politique*, IIIe Essai, p. 170.

Sismondi had resumed the debate, begun by the Physiocrats and now participated in with great zeal by increasing numbers of economists and political theorists. More and more alarmed by the effects of *morcellement* [62] and impressed with the need of capital and up-to-date techniques in agriculture, the advocates of large-scale farming repeated all of the arguments of its British exponents. These were countered with determination by the adherents of family farming. Every aspect of the question, political, social, economic and moral, was treated in detail by writers like Hippolyte Passy, de Foville, Léon Faucher, Léonce de Lavergne, and Le Play.[63] In his *Des Systèmes de Culture en France et de Leur Influence sur l'Economie Sociale* (1852), Passy conceded that there were many diverse factors in determining the optimum size and type of farm, such as the political system, the size and density of the population, the distribution of wealth, climate, and topography, and the supply of land, but concluded in favor of *la petite culture* as the most productive and profitable economically. Politically and socially it was likewise to be preferred, since it preserved the greatest degree of independence and freedom for the individual and kept the greatest number of people on the land. The latter was especially desirable because the agricultural population of a country was more robust, saner, and more stable than the manufacturing.[64] More often than not the argument turned

62. *Morcellement* and *parcellement* may be understood as synonyms for the reduction of large into small units of property, though the former has the particular meaning of dividing large into smaller contiguous units, whereas *parcellement* properly means dividing them into scattered, noncontiguous units. Cf. Vandervynckt, E., *Le Remembrement parmi les Améliorations Foncières Rurales*, Paris, 1936, p. 8.
63. Cf. Augé-Laribé, *Grande ou Petite Prop.*, Ch. III.
64. *Ibid.*, pp. 79-89.

on these non-economic considerations, and invariably tended to favor the small family farm.

The entrance of the socialists into the debate drove both liberal and conservative economists—and consistent political majorities—into the arms of the peasants. The Marxists' interpretation, and solution, of the agrarian problem was a projection of their scheme for the reorganization of industrial society. As evident from his commendation of the *bourgeoisie*, in the Communist Manifesto, for having built up the cities and "thus rescued a considerable part of the population from the idiocy of rural life," [65] and from his dilations on the miseries of the British peasantry, in *Capital*, Marx himself found no particular virtues in the agrarian way of life and considered the average farmer as palpable a victim of exploitation as the proletarian worker. According to him, there was a fundamental conflict between rural and urban life that could only be resolved by the class struggle and the amalgamation of the peasants in the industrial proletariat. That was their proper place. They were kept out of it by their possession of property, which aligned their sympathies with the *petite bourgeoisie*. But this property did not give them real independence. They enjoyed the illusion of social independence, but economically they were subject to the "exploitation" of the market, whose price they could not control; of usury, in the form of mortgages; and of landlord and employer in case they were tenants and full- or part-time laborers. [66]

65. Text from *Handbook of Marxism*, New York, 1935, p. 27.
66. See the full account of Marx's agrarian ideas, including extensive passages from his works, in Augé-Laribé, *Grande ou Petite Propriété*, Ch. IV; also *Karl Marx und die Agrarfrage*, Moscow, 1933, esp. Sennow, A., "Zur Frage des Gegensatzes zwischen Stadt und Land und seiner Aufhebung," and Baryschew, N., "Marx über den Gross und Kleinbetrieb in der Landwirtschaft," pp. 69-110, 224-267.

As to the relative merits of large and small farms, both were cursed by private ownership, which made the large proprietor the instrument of the exploitations affecting small proprietor, tenant, or laborer. Otherwise, large farms were to be preferred. Small family farms, with their attendant evil of *parcellement*, were the ruination of the French peasant. They prevented the accumulation of capital and the application of scientific techniques and kept their owners in poverty. Sold in small parcels, the price of land could be bid up far in excess of its cost in large masses and of its true productive value.

> Small peasants' property excludes by its very nature the development of the social powers of production of labor, the social forms of labor, the social concentration of capitals, cattle raising on a large scale, and a progressive application of science.
>
> Usury and a system of taxation must impoverish it everywhere. The expenditure of capital in the price of land withdraws this capital from cultivation. An infinite dissipation of means of production and an isolation of the producers themselves go with it. Also an enormous waste of human energy. A progressive deterioration of the conditions of production and a raising of the price of means of production is a necessary law of small peasants' property. Fertile seasons are a misfortune for this mode of production.[67]

It prevented division of labor and mechanization. It was compatible only with a primitive state of production. To perpetuate it would be "to decree mediocrity in everything." [68] The small peasant landowner had fulfilled his role as the conqueror of feudalism; he should now pool his property and his fortunes in the collectivized, classless society of socialism. All landed property should be nationalized and agricultural production organized in large units. This was the agrarian

---

67. From Marx, Karl, *Capital*, Chicago, 1909, Vol. III, Part VI, Chap. XLVII, p. 938; Augé-Laribé, *op. cit.*, p. 115.
68. *Idem.*

book of Marxism, the final page of which has yet to be written in Soviet Russia.[69]

When it came to putting these ideas into practice, however, French socialists made the same discovery aristocrats and republicans had made before them: that the customs of the peasants were stronger than political or economic theory. They soon realized that they would have to draw in their horns if they were to stand any chance of winning the peasants to their cause. Accordingly, at a party congress at Marseilles, in 1892, Paul Lafargue and Jules Guesde collaborated on an agrarian program that affirmed the Marxist principle of the inevitable disappearance of peasant property. But they promised the peasants not only exemption from the socialization of the land, which was to apply only to large landowners, but also protection to farmers and share-croppers who improved the value of the land of others.[70] Engels promptly denounced these qualifications as incompatible with socialist principles, but they remained a fundamental part of French socialism.

In the periodic debates in the Chamber of Deputies, at party congresses, everywhere they turned, the socialists encountered the mobilized partisans of the family farm. In 1896 a league for the protection of peasant farming was formed, with a journal entitled *La Petite Propriété*. The Société des Agriculteurs de France lent its support to the organization of rural syndicates as much to resist socialism as to promote technical reforms. At a congress of the Union of these syndicates, in 1897, a motion to reduce *morcellement*

69. For the application of Marx's theories to Russian agriculture see esp. Rochester, Anna, *Lenin on the Agrarian Question*, New York, 1942; Bienstock, G., Schwarz, S. M., and Yugow, A., *Management in Russian Industry and Agriculture*, New York, 1944, Chs. X-XVII; and Baykov, A., *The Development of the Soviet Economic System*, Cambridge, 1946, Chs. XII, XVII.
70. Augé-Laribé, *Grande et Petite Prop.*, pp. 130-132.

and encourage large and medium-sized farms was rejected in
favor of one that concluded:

> You oppose to socialism a barrier that it will not be able to sur-
> mount. Its propaganda, so facile among the proletarians of the city
> or the factory, will get nowhere with the *petits propriétaires* if they
> are firmly established on the soil which they wish to leave to their
> children. They are the best support of the social order and our
> syndicates constitute the best organized force to defend it.[71]

Réné Henry, whose work *La Petite Propriété Rurale en
France* (1895) was used as ammunition against the socialist
Juares, held likewise that the peasants were the sturdiest,
healthiest, most enlightened members of society, that they
made the best soldiers, and that the system of family farms
and small holdings was best because it kept their number at
its greatest strength.[72] Against this stubborn current, French
socialists made little headway. Nor did the Communists, with
their Confédération Générale des Paysans Travailleurs, organized in 1929, succeed where the socialists had failed. Both
parties were repeatedly forced to compromise the principles
of Marxism, to guarantee the peasant his property in order
to win his support.[73]

The guarantee was renewed by the Communists in 1945.
Their agrarian platform was of more than ordinary interest,
not only because of the decisive role they played in French
politics in that year but also because of their widespread
strength in rural provinces. Drawn up at the party congress
in Paris (June 26-30, 1945), it called for a wholesale modernization of French agriculture, including *remembrement*

71. *Ibid.*, p. 143.
72. *Ibid.*, p. 171.
73. Cf. Augé-Laribé, *L'Evolution de la France Agricole*, Paris, 1912,
    Ch. VII; *Le Paysan Français après la Guerre*, Paris, 1923, pp.
    192-207, 280 ff.; Hunter, Neil, *Peasantry and Crisis in France*,
    London, 1938, pp. 243 ff.; Yates, *Food Production*, pp. 303-308,
    330.

and the introduction of long-overdue technical and economic reforms. At the same time it endorsed the family farm as "the dominant form of our French agricultural economy," to which all reforms and improvements would have to conform.[74] The Constitution of 1946 renewed the guarantees of private property implicit in this resolution, in which the farthest left of all French parties found common ground with its enemies. But the Communists would not admit it. They claimed that the record of their members in the Constituent Assembly in 1945 and 1946 proved them "the most ardent of all defenders of *la petite et moyenne propriété paysanne.*" [75]

For a time, economic trends and policies combined with agrarian tradition to fortify the position of the small peasant farm and its defenders. During the mid-century, the extensive construction of railways, improvements in agricultural technology, and the stimulus given to exports by a series of reciprocal trade treaties (1860-1867) brought about considerable agricultural prosperity. Though interrupted by the Franco-Prussian War, this lasted until late in the seventies, when the competition of American and other non-European

74. The particular planks dealing with this question read as follows:
   "Pour diverses raisons d'ordre économique et social particulières à la France, nous considerons que l'exploitation familiale, qui n'est d'ailleurs pas incompatible avec le progrès de l'agriculture, restera pendant longtemps encore la forme dominante de notre économie agricole française.
   "C'est pourquoi, l'industrie de la machine agricole que nous devons créer doit être conçue, non en fonction de la très grande culture, comme c'est le cas aux Etats-Unis ou en U.R.S.S., mais en vue de produire un matériel qui s'adapte à l'étendue de nos exploitations. (Applaudissements)." Rochet, Waldek, *Pour la Restauration de l'Agriculture Française*, Xe Congrès National du Parti Communiste Français, Paris, 26-30 Juin 1945, p. 21.
75. *Le Bilan des Elus Communistes en faveur des Paysans*, April, 1946, p. 9.

grains and meat that affected British farmers so drastically was felt in France in the same way. Abrogation of the trade treaties and the resumption of protection was immediately demanded. Comprehensive agricultural and industrial tariffs were imposed in 1885, and France has remained protectionist ever since.[76] She was one of the first European powers to raise her agricultural tariffs after the First World War (1927), and with the advent of the depression she supplemented these with the same paraphernalia of subsidies, import quotas, price-fixing, crop and marketing controls as the British and, subsequently, the American.[77]

These protectionist policies tended, as always, to preserve the agricultural *status quo*, the existing allocation of resources, peasant farming, *parcellement*, and all the rest of it. How deliberately solicitous of the family farm they were may be inferred from a law of 1931 limiting the production of wine. This was characteristically a family enterprise, and to keep it that way and protect it from the competition of the relatively few large-scale producers, the planting of new vines by owners of vineyards over 25 acres in size was prohibited. Small farmers were the prime movers and specific beneficiaries of the entire related program of public and co-operative credit agencies, co-operative purchasing and marketing associations, dairies, wine presses, and flour mills, and the scores of agricultural societies that sprang up in France toward the turn of the century, whose collective membership ran into the millions by 1929. They used these devices as individuals, as means to ends, with jealous regard to local initiative. In this sense they proved the accuracy of Marx's assertion that "capitalistic co-operation does not manifest itself as a particular historical form of co-operation, but co-operation itself appears to be a historical form peculiar to, and

76. Viallate, *op. cit.*, pp. 194 ff., 265-277, 381-386.
77. *Ibid.*, pp. 433-436; Yates, *op. cit.*, pp. 311-323.

specifically distinguishing, the capitalist process of production." [78] And if the financial test be applied, the peasants never permitted their indebtedness to all credit agencies, public, private and co-operative, to go as high as 25 per cent of their aggregate capital [79]—a striking contrast with Great Britain and the United States. [80]

This individualism and political strength of the peasants showed up even more vividly in the face of the government's efforts at *remembrement*, the consolidation, or regrouping, of scattered parcels into larger, integral units of production. This policy had been advocated by economists as a corrective to *parcellement* since Arthur Young's time, and during the latter half of the nineteenth century various attempts were made—such as reducing the tax on exchanges of noncontiguous for contiguous property—to put it into effect. [81] They came to nothing. The peasants stubbornly opposed any change and were suspicious of the slightest hint of an attack on the law of equal inheritance. Moreover, the ardor of the reformers was dampened, first by the general agricultural prosperity, and then by the economic advantages that seemed to accrue to the small family farm in the hard times that followed it. The combination of falling agricultural prices and the draining off of agricultural labor into the factories weighed heavily on large-scale commercial farmers, both in the last quarter of the nineteenth century and again in the period of scarce labor and high wages after the First World War. In these circumstances the family farmer often fared better than the employer and market producer. [82] *Remembrement* was wholly consistent with, and indeed solicitous of,

78. *Capital*, Modern Library Ed., p. 367.
79. Yates, *op. cit.*, p. 290.
80. Cf. p. 78 above.
81. Vandervynkt, E., *Le Remembrement parmi les Améliorations Foncières Rurales*, Paris, 1936, pp. 68 ff., 134-169.
82. *Ibid.*, pp. 31-33; Viallate, *op. cit.*, p. 337.

family farming, but it implied change and that was distasteful to the peasants, even in the form of improvement. As a member of the Chamber of Deputies despairingly said of the small farmer in 1916, "experience shows that habit often paralyzes him and that his interest, which he sometimes understands very poorly, does not suffice to govern his conduct." [83]

Not until 1918 was a general policy of *remembrement* initiated by legislation. Military necessity now lent its weight to the arguments of the economists. France was fighting with her back to the wall, and the need for food was urgent. *Remembrement* was now advocated as a means of increasing the food supply by consolidating the small parcels, on which the intensive use of agricultural machinery was impossible, into units suitable to this type of cultivation. Even so, it was strenuously resisted. The Deputies were reminded that the peasants had "a very narrow conception of the right of property, of *dominium:* a man's house is his castle." France was "above all a country of small farms and *petits propriétaires;* that is its originality and its strength." *Morcellement* was not an accident but a "natural fact," and as such, though it might be reduced, it could not be abolished. "One may correct nature but not transform her by violating her." A law might be necessary, but it would have to conform "in perfect harmony with our national institutions and the principles of our legislation." [84] That the French could tarry over such considerations with the Germans hammering at their gates shows at least how seriously they took them.

The protracted debate, which began early in 1917, finally resulted in two laws (November 27, 1918, and March 4,

83. Vandervynkt, *op. cit.*, p. 179.
84. *Ibid.*, pp. 199, 213.   These sentiments were echoed with great emotion by writers like Labat, E., *L'Ame Paysanne*, Paris, 1923, and Roupnel, G., *Histoire de la Campagne Française*, Paris, 1932.

1919). The first, which was nation-wide in scope, merely created legal machinery for use in cases in which *remembrement* was desired and the free exchange of parcels proved impossible. It provided that a majority of the landowners concerned might appoint a commission, presided over by a justice of the peace, and composed of local officials and representatives of the interested landowners elected from their own number, to plan and supervise the project. The majority was given the right to constrain the minority in principle, but no sanctions or means of coercion other than arbitration, persuasion, and the ordinary recourse to law. This law proved so weak and ineffectual that by 1934 only 93 *remembrements* had been initiated under its terms, of which 39 had been abandoned, 44 were in progress, and only 10 completed.[85] The law of 1919, which applied to war-devastated areas only, was much more effective. It vested real authority in the departmental prefect, who, with the advice and assistance of a communal commission, consisting of the justice of the peace of the canton, the mayor of the local village, technical experts, and six landowners appointed by the prefect from a list approved by all the landowners concerned, could plan and execute the *remembrement* by the administrative process. Full opportunities for hearings and adjudications were provided, and by a supplementary law of April 17, the state assumed all expenses incurred. Under this law, 376 *remembrements* had been completed by 1934 and 128 more were in progress.[86] But it was a temporary relief measure, limited in scope and owing a large part of its success to the preliminary destruction of vested interests by the war.

From time to time attempts were made to strengthen the law of 1918, the results of which were disappointing. At length the law was superseded by a decree of October 30,

85. *Ibid.*, pp. 245-246. Text of laws, pp. 353-360.
86. *Ibid.*, pp. 271-290, 352.

1935, which, though it did not go as far as the law of 1919, was an improvement on that of 1918. It left much the same degree of initiative with the local landowners in starting a *remembrement* project, but created smoother and more effective administrative machinery for carrying it out once it was under way. For example, it replaced the four representatives of the interested landowners on the communal commission with six landowners having no interest in the project, to be appointed by the departmental chamber of agriculture; and it canceled the privilege of withdrawal on the part of dissatisfied owners whose possessions lay within the perimeter of the *remembrement*. Still, it followed the laissez-faire line and left the initiative with the individual landowners of each local community.[87]

None of these laws touched the problem of equal inheritance, which, as we have noted, combined with the man-land ratio to produce *parcellement*. In 1938 the Civil Code was modified so as to make it possible to keep a rural estate intact upon the decease of its owner. This did not disturb the principle of equal inheritance. It merely simplified the procedure whereby a single heir might take possession of an entire, undivided estate by agreement with his co-heirs.[88] These inheritance laws, like the *remembrement* laws, were permissive rather than obligatory, and all of them together were suspended by the coming of the Second World War. They

87. Text of decree, *ibid.*, pp. 360-375.
88. This was accomplished by laws of February 7 and June 17, 1938. The latter provided that farms valued at less than 200,000 francs might remain undivided for a period of five years in spite of the opposition of a co-heir if such was the desire of surviving spouse or heir (if under age), and the period could be renewed until the decease of the spouse or until the heir came of age. For text and terms see Duvergier, J. B., ed., *Collection Complète des Lois*, 1938, Series II, Vol. XXXVIII, pp. 141 ff.; Spiegel, Henry W., *Land Tenure Policies at Home and Abroad*, Chapel Hill, 1941, p. 24.

made slight impression on the vast acreage, officially estimated at no less than one-quarter of the total agricultural
land of France, in which *parcellement* had been carried beyond the point of diminishing returns.[89]

It is interesting to compare these latter-day trends in
French agricultural policy with those already observed in
Britain. In that they fostered, and established uniform procedures for, converting small parcels into larger farms, they
resembled the British enclosure acts of the early nineteenth
century. On the other hand, they contrasted sharply with the
British allotments and small-holdings policy that coincided
with them. The purpose of the British policy was to resettle
people on the land in small agricultural units. The French
were trying to do exactly the opposite, to recruit their industrial labor force from their surplus agricultural population
and establish the portion of the latter that remained on the
land in larger productive units.[90] Once again the contrast
presents itself of a nation that discounted the cultural and
political value of family farming and the agrarian way of
life, with one that placed the highest emphasis upon it—both,
it should be noted, in the name of democracy.

Whatever the spiritual results of this French policy, the
reform of its material consequences was placed high on the
agenda of the coalition government in 1946. The excessively
large agricultural population, crowded onto its tiny parcels,
and cherishing its ancient ways, had unquestionably retarded
the industrial and commercial development of the country
and depressed its general standard of living. To a degree

89. Augé-Laribé, "Structure Agricole," *loc. cit.*, pp. 126-127; Yates,
    op. cit., p. 281. The Communist Party estimated the number of
    parcels at 125,000,000 in 1945. Rochet, Waldek, *Pour la Res-
    tauration*, p. 20.
90. On the other hand, the Communists favored breaking up large
    holdings not actively farmed by their owners and selling them in
    smaller units to active farmers. Cf. Rochet, *op. cit.*, pp. 22-23.

perhaps unique among rural populations, it had contributed
to the decline in the national birth rate, as parents hoarded
their meager properties and strained them through the sieve
of equal inheritance.[91] To millions of its own number it had
brought wretched material returns: poor houses, inadequate
schools, and a rural death rate that had exceeded the urban
since 1901 and bespoke the lack of medical services and hospitals.[92] It had given France self-sufficiency in foodstuffs with
a wastage of productive resources that may be imagined from
the fact that a single agricultural producer feeds only 5 consumers in France, as compared with 15 in the United States.[93]
The plain implication of these statistics and of the economic
policies contemplated by the government in 1946 was that
agrarianism and individualism had been carried too far. Plans
were being made for an intensive program of industrialization and foreign trade, modernization of agriculture, *remembrement*, and the reduction of the working agricultural population by as much as 2,000,000 [94]—objectives to which the
British had committed themselves in 1846, exactly a hundred
years before.

The ills these policies were designed to remedy could not
be charged entirely to family farming. The million of
France's four million agricultural holdings under 2½ acres
in size were not farms. Neither were many of the 1,860,000

91. According to Clapham (*Economic Development of France and
Germany*, p. 160), "It could in fact be said with almost absolute
truth that population has not grown in order that holdings might
not be subdivided . . ." Cf. Augé-Laribé, *L'Evolution de la
France Agricole*, p. 137, and other French authorities cited in
Great Britain, *Reports from Commissioners*, 1. "Agriculture,"
Vol. VII, 1924, "France," p. 291.

92. Cf. Yates, *op. cit.*, pp. 294-303.

93. France. Gouvernement Provisoire de la République Française,
Commissariat Général de Plan de Modernisation et d'Equipement,
*Statistical Review of the Economic and Financial Situation of
France at the Beginning of 1946*, Paris, 1946, p. 7.

94. Cf. *ibid.*, pp. 3-16.

under 25 acres.[95] It was the perversion of family farming of which Arthur Young spoke at the time of the Revolution, when he said that forty or fifty acres were "not incapable of good husbandry; but when divided, twenty acres *must* be ill-cultivated; again divided, they become farms of ten acres, or five, of two . . . and even a quarter of a rood, with a family as much attached to it as if it were a hundred acres"; [96] and Augé-Laribé, in 1939, when he declared that the "democratic" division of agricultural property had been carried to excess.[97] These conditions resulted from a corruption of the Jeffersonian ideal rather than its fulfillment, from the exaggeration of its several elements: individualism, agrarianism, *laisser faire, laisser passer*. It is true that the conditions formed the foundation of folkway and custom upon which the democratic political structure was erected. Yet their contributions to the solidity and strength of the latter might have been greater than is indicated by the record of French democracy as a system of government, with its 14 constitutions since 1789 and its 106 cabinets from 1870 to 1940,[98] and by the self-questionings and plans for reform of that system in 1946. Democracy, as the French construed it—in the fierce light of individualism—enabled the peasants to maintain their own *ancien régime* long past its time. French agrarianism, amounting to a national passion, partaking more of romance than political economy, encouraged its preservation. The tradition of laissez faire and the strict construction of the property right kept hands off the museum.

Great Britain ignored the Jeffersonian ideal. France distorted it. It is now time to turn back and see how it fared in the United States.

95. Cf. p. 88 above.
96. Cf. p. 104 above.
97. Cf. p. 88 above.
98. Cf. Franck, Louis R., "The Future of Representative Democracy in France," *Foreign Affairs*, 1946, Vol. XXIV, p. 224.

CHAPTER FIVE

The American Policy

IF ARTHUR YOUNG could have extended his travels to the United States during its first century of independence, he would have discovered a system of farming and land tenure that contrasted with the British no less strikingly than did the French. This is how it appeared to one of his countrymen, First Secretary of the British Legation in Washington in 1869:

The system of land occupation in the United States of America may be generally described as by small proprietors.

The proprietary class throughout the country is, moreover, rapidly on the increase, whilst that of the tenancy is diminishing and is principally supplied by immigration.

The theory and practice of the country is for every man to own land as soon as possible.

The term of landlord is an obnoxious one.

The American people are very averse to being tenants and are anxious to be masters of the soil. . . .

The possession of land of itself does not bestow on a man, as it does in Europe, a title to consideration; indeed, its possession in large quantities frequently reacts prejudicially to his interests as attaching to him a taint of aristocracy which is distasteful to the masses of the American people. . . .

It may be asserted that the system of land-tenure by small proprietors is regarded in this country with great favour, and that the prevailing public opinion is that the possession of land should be within the reach of the most modest means.

A proprietor of land, however small, acquires a stake in the country, and assumes responsibilities which guarantee his discharging faithfully his duties as a citizen.

As previously stated, tenancy cannot be said to exist as a system in the United States.[1]

From these detached observations—part of a contemporary British Foreign Office investigation of European and American systems of agriculture and land tenure—it is clear that up to the last quarter of the nineteenth century the American system was still essentially the Jeffersonian. The disintegration of that system into the conditions described by the President's Committee on Farm Tenancy in 1937 kept pace with the industrial revolution in the United States. We have already taken account of the main effects of the industrial revolution on American agriculture. We have observed the decisive role that revolution played in England and its less decisive role in France. To perceive its results more clearly in the United States the reader will again find statistics more helpful than words. From 1870, the year following the British Legation Secretary's report, to 1945, the year of the most recent agricultural census, our farm population declined from 75 to 17 per cent of the total population, and the number of persons employed in agriculture, from 53 to less than 15 per cent of the working population.[2] In round numbers, the farm population dropped from a peak of 32,000,000 in 1910 to 23,500,000 in 1945, and the number of persons

1. Great Britain, *Accounts and Papers*, 1870, Vol. LXVII, pp. 465-466, 477.
2. Wright, C. W., *Economic History of the United States*, New York, 1941, pp. 643-645; Gee, Wilson, *The Social Economics of Agriculture*, New York, 1942, pp. 388-394; Barger and Landsberg, *American Agriculture*, p. 299; Shannon, Fred A., *The Farmer's Last Frontier*, New York, 1945, pp. 349-352. Census returns and Bureau of Agricultural Economics Estimates from Barger and Landsberg, *op. cit.*, pp. 230-246, 298-300; U. S. Department of Commerce, Bureau of the Census, *Series-Census-BAE*, No. 7, May 2, 1946; Department of Agriculture, *Agricultural Statistics*, 1944, p. 406; Schultz, T. W., *Agriculture in an Unstable Economy*, New York, 1945, Ch. IV.

employed in agriculture, from 11,500,000 to 8,200,000. The number of farms remained around 6,300,000 from 1910 to 1930, touched its peak of slightly more than 6,800,000 during the depression, then dropped to 5,800,000 in 1945.[3] These figures show at a glance the extent to which the total structure of American democracy had outgrown its agrarian foundations.

The statistics are not so clear as to what this meant for the family farm. "Is the so-called family-size farm passing from the American scene?," the New York *Times* inquired editorially in the winter of 1947, "Or is it just getting larger than it used to be?" The editorial writer had the final returns of the 1945 Census of Agriculture before him, but he could do no better with them than conclude that perhaps both trends were in progress.[4] It was plain, at all events, that technology had greatly increased the productivity of American agriculture and caused the same redundancy of farm labor it had caused everywhere else.[5] It increased the average size of all American farms from 138.1 acres in 1910 to 194.8 acres

	1910	1930	1940	1945
Total farm population	32,077,000	30,445,000	30,547,000	23,558,000
No. of persons employed in agriculture	11,592,000	10,472,000	9,163,000	8,200,000
No. of farms	6,361,000	6,288,000	6,096,000	5,859,000

3. Figures for 1910, 1930, and 1940 from detailed analysis of employment in agriculture, based on Bureau of Agricultural Economics estimates and census returns in Barger and Landsberg, *op. cit.*, pp. 228-246. All figures in first two categories are for April. Farm population for 1945 from *U.S. Census of Agriculture, 1945*. Employment in agriculture for 1945 and all figures on number of farms from *Statistical Abstract of the U.S., 1946*, p. 173. See also *America's Needs and Resources*, J. Frederick Dewhurst and Associates, New York, 1947, pp. 40-41, 620-621.

4. New York *Times*, Feb. 17, 1947.

5. Cf. Hopkins, John A., *Changing Technology and Employment in Agriculture*, U.S. Department of Agriculture, Bureau of Agricultural Economics, Washington, 1941.

in 1945.[6] Of late years, technology and commerce together
have given such an impetus to large-scale commercial farming
as to suggest a modern American enclosure movement that
would swallow up family farming as it did in England.[7]

At first glance, the statistics seem to make the possibility
a probability. From 1920 to 1940, farms of 1,000 acres and
over (the largest category designated in the census returns)
increased from 23.1 to 34.3 per cent of the total land in
farms, and from 1 to 1.6 per cent of their total number.[8]

6. U.S. Dept. of Commerce, Bureau of the Census, *Statistical Ab-
stract of the U.S., 1946*, p. 573; *U.S. Census of Agriculture, 1945*.
7. See esp. McWilliams, Carey, *Factories in the Fields*, Boston, 1939;
Ill Fares the Land, Boston, 1942; and *Small Farm and Big Farm*,
New York, Public Affairs Committee Pamphlet No. 100, 1945.
Also U.S. Department of Commerce, Bureau of the Census, and
Department of Agriculture, Bureau of Agricultural Economics,
Large-Scale Farming in the United States, Washington, 1929;
Temporary National Economic Committee, *Agriculture and the
National Economy*, Monograph No. 23, Washington, 1940.
8. *Stat. Abstr. of the U.S., 1946*, p. 574.

	Per cent dis-tribution of num-ber of farms		Per cent dis-tribution of land in farms	
	1920	1940	1920	1940
Under 3 acres	.3	.6	*	*
3 to 9 acres	4.2	7.7	.2	.2
10 to 19 acres	7.9	9.2	.7	.7
20 to 49 acres	23.3	20.0	5.1	3.8
50 to 99 acres	22.9	21.2	11.1	8.8
100 to 499 acres	38.1	37.0	49.3	41.6
500 to 999 acres	2.3	2.7	10.6	10.6
1,000 acres and over	1.0	1.6	23.1	34.3

* Less than one-tenth of one per cent.

	1920	1940
No. of farms of 1,000 acres and over	67,405	100,531
All land in farms of 1,000 acres and over (1,000's of acres)	220,636	364,069

Wartime production schedules accelerated these trends, increasing
1,000-acre and larger farms from 34.3% in 1940 to 40.3% in
1945 of the total land in farms, and from 1.6% in 1940 to 1.9%
of the total number of farms in the U.S. in 1945. *U.S. Census of
Agriculture, 1945*.

Meanwhile farms of all smaller-size groups remained constant, or declined both in number and in aggregate percentage of the total farm land. But size is not an infallible distinction between large-scale and family farming. Though most farms of 1,000 acres or more may safely be placed in the former category, identifying a farm of smaller dimensions in any such diversified agricultural system as the American depends largely upon its crop and region. Seven or eight hundred acres might easily represent a family farm in the Dakotas or a large-scale enterprise in Pennsylvania.

Broken down by regions, the census figures show that the gains of large-scale farming have been heavily concentrated in the West, particularly in the Pacific (especially California) and Mountain (especially Arizona and New Mexico) states, and are not a nation-wide phenomenon. They represent an expansion of this type of farming in areas where it already prevailed—in crops and livestock such as citrus fruit, wheat, and cattle, that are universally adapted to large-scale cultivation and production—rather than conquests in the domain of family farming. Thus from 1920 to 1940 the percentage of total farm land in farms of 1,000 acres and over declined or increased only slightly in every region except the Pacific, Mountain, and West North Central.[9] The same is true of the

9. Table from Temporary National Economic Committee Monograph No. 23, *Agriculture and the National Economy*, 1940, p. 10; 1940 percentages computed from 1940 census, Vol. III, *Agriculture*, pp. 84-88.

Region	1920	1930	1940
New England	4.7	4.4	2.9
Middle Atlantic	2.4	1.7	2.3
East North Central	1.2	1.1	1.2
West North Central	16.7	17.1	23
South Atlantic	9.2	7.7	12
East South Central	6.1	5.0	6.7
West South Central	41.1	40.3	46.
Mountain	52.3	60.9	78.
Pacific	50.1	51.9	62.

substantial increase in the average size of farms during the Second World War. From 1940 to 1945 this average rose from 174 to 194.8 acres. But the average was a composite of regional increases, ranging from 35.1 per cent in the Mountain states to 0.5 in the Middle Atlantic and −8.4 (a decline) in New England.[10]

The 1945 Census of Agriculture explains these increases as follows:

About three-fourths of the increase in land in farms occurred in the Western States. This increase was largely the result of the inclusion, as land in farms, of grazing land not reported in previous censuses as land in farms. Also, the 1945 acreage included more Indian grazing lands than in 1940, because of the changes in the method of enumerating agricultural operations on Indian reservations. In censuses prior to 1945, much of the grazing land on Indian reservations was not counted as land in farms as it was considered open range. Likewise, the change in the method of enumerating operations of Indian farmers affected the number of farms. In 1945, where the acreage on reservations was used on a cooperative basis, an Indian reservation was reported as a single farm. Consequently, the 1945 Census of Agriculture shows a reduction in the number of farms in areas where there are Indians and an increase in land in farms in the same areas.[11]

10. Table from U.S. Dept. of Commerce, Bureau of the Census, *1945 Census of Agriculture, Preliminary,* Nov. 30, 1945, p. 2.

Region	Average Acreage 1945	Average Acreage 1940	Per cent change
New England	90.6	98.9	−8.4
Middle Atlantic	97.1	96.6	0.5
East North Central	111.4	113.0	5.7
West North Central	272.8	251.6	8.4
South Atlantic	93.0	90.8	2.4
East South Central	78.0	75.3	3.6
West South Central	228.5	207.9	9.9
Mountain	1,110.5	821.9	35.1
Pacific	246.4	230.6	6.9

11. *U.S. Census of Agriculture, 1945,* p. 3.

Rich or poor, productive or unproductive, the overwhelming majority of American farms continued to be operated as family ventures.[12]

Measuring farms by their income leads to the same conclusions. In a classification in favor with the Department of Agriculture, a family farm is one that grosses a minimum of $600, and a maximum of $10,000, a year (in 1939 purchasing power), in general terms, "a farm on which the operator, devoting substantially full time to farming operations, with the help of other members of his family and without employing more than a moderate amount of outside labor, can make a satisfactory living and maintain the farm plant." [13] Anything below the minimum was by definition a residential, part-time, or subsistence farm; anything above the maximum, a large-scale commercial farm. According to this classifica-

---

12. It is interesting to compare the average size of farms in North and East in 1860 with that in 1945. Representative state figures were:

	Average size in acres	
	1860	1945
Massachusetts	93.8	46.0
Connecticut	99.5	69.6
Ohio	113.8	97.5
Illinois	145.9	153.2
Iowa	164.6	164.1

Figures from Bidwell, P. W., and Falconer, J. I., *History of Agriculture in the Northern United States, 1620-1860,* Washington, 1925, p. 449; *1945 Census of Agriculture, Preliminary,* Nov. 30, 1945. Gray, L. C., *History of Agriculture in the Southern United States to 1860,* 2 vols., Washington, 1933, Vol. I, p. 452, says that plantations never exceeded 18% of the total farms of the South.

13. Department of Agriculture, Interbureau Committee on Postwar Agricultural Problems, *Farm Opportunities in the United States,* Washington, July, 1945, pp. 110, 44-45. The classification was suggested by Benedict, M. R., etc., "Need for a New Classification of Farms," *Journal of Farm Economics,* 1944, Vol. XXVI, pp. 694-708.

tion, there were 3,125,000 family farms in the United States in 1940, 2,345,000 lesser-than-family farms, and only 80,000 large-scale commercial farms.[14] Although 42 per cent of our farms failed to qualify as family farms by these economic standards, by far the largest part were family farms in a sociological sense, and the two groups together constituted all but a small fraction of the total.[15]

An even more obvious indication of the extent of family farming is the ratio of farmers to farms. By the most generous calculation, a family farm can employ no more than the farmer's family and "a moderate amount of outside labor." With a total farm employment of approximately 8,200,000 distributed among slightly less than 6,000,000 farms, it is evident that not many could exceed the family category in economic, much less in sociological, dimensions.[16] The fact becomes more clear in contrast with the distribution

14. Representing, respectively, 56.3%, 42% and 1.4% of a total of 5,550,000 farms excluding share-croppers. *Farm Opportunities*, p. 45.

15. A 1945 estimate placed the number of family farms at 4,262,172, lesser-than-family farms at 1,500,360, and large-scale farms at 289,040, representing respectively 70%, 25%, and 5% of the total number of farms. *U.S. Census of Agriculture, 1945*, March, 1947, p. 5.

16.

Year	Total employment	No. of farms
1930	10,472,000	6,288,648
1940	9,163,000	6,096,799
1945	8,200,000	5,859,169

Figures from Barger and Landsberg, *op. cit.*, p. 231; *Statistical Abstract, 1946*, p. 573; *U.S. Census of Agriculture, 1945*. See also Dewhurst, *op. cit.*, pp. 620-621. It has been estimated that in 1935 not more than 42,000 out of nearly 7,000,000 farms employed more than 5 persons. National Resources Board, *The Structure of the American Economy*, Washington, 1939, Part I, p. 103.

of industrial labor: in manufacturing alone, 7,886,567 wage earners to 184,230 factories in 1939.[17]

Relative to the other branches of the economy, agriculture remained the domain of small-scale individual enterprise, that was clear. But it was not altogether free enterprise, for it had made its terms with both business and government. Certainly agriculture could no longer be considered the unique abode of democracy. If it were, democracy was beyond the reach of four-fifths of the American people, for less than a fifth of them were farmers. Even among that fifth there were so many tenants and mortgages that the integrity and independence that Jefferson believed to be imbued in the husbandman by the care of his own fields could no longer be taken for granted. Those qualities, and the property right that was supposed to guarantee them to society, derived in the first instance from economic independence; and economic independence, defined with any regard to the ethical pretensions of modern society or the material capacities of its technology, was many times more difficult of attainment by the modern farmer than it had been by his ancestor. It was no longer to be had for the clearing of wilderness or prairie. In Jefferson's time a family farmer could write:

At this time, my farm gave me and my whole family a good living on the produce of it; and left me, one year with another, one hundred and fifty silver dollars, for I have never spent more than ten dollars a year, which was for salt, nails and the like. Nothing to wear, eat, or drink, was purchased, as my farm provided all. With this saving, I put money to interest, bought cattle, fatted and sold them, and made great profit.[18]

17. This was the average number of wage earners for the year. *Stat. Abstr., 1946*, p. 809. Cf. Barger and Landsberg, *op. cit.*, pp. 3 ff.
18. Quoted by Gray, *op. cit.*, p. 452.

A self-sufficient farm in our time is more likely to be a haunt of illiteracy and malnutrition than a wellspring of democracy.

This was the great change that the industrial revolution had wrought in American agriculture: it had either drawn the family farm into its orbit or left it stranded in an archaic subsistence economy. In 1945, 80 per cent of our agricultural commodities were produced by the top third (50 per cent by the top tenth) of our farms, 16 per cent by the middle third, and only 4 per cent by the lowest third.[19] To qualify as such by modern standards, a family farmer had to compromise his Jeffersonian independence of commerce and industry and look to the *deus ex machina* in Washington as well as "to heaven and his own soil and industry."

The extent of his dependence on business and business-men, not only for the necessities of life and the tools of his trade but also for the marketing of his products, is suggested by 1934 and 1935 figures showing that the nation's five lead-ing meat packers purchased and slaughtered 66.2 per cent of its meat animals; its three leading dairy companies pur-chased and distributed 16 per cent of its fluid milk and cream, 21 per cent of its butter, and 63 per cent of its cheese; and its three leading flour-milling companies purchased and milled 29 per cent of its wheat.[20] Canning companies, chain stores, and terminal markets had even robbed the highly decen-tralized production of fruits and vegetables of its immunity to monopoly. All of these enterprises together took the func-tions of processing and distributing away from the farmer, leaving him the sole function of production, and dictating his rewards for that. He had to do business with business. Even

19. See *U.S. Census of Agriculture, 1945*, March, 1947, esp. p. 8, and *The Agricultural Situation*, March, 1947, pp. 1-4.
20. Statistics from Hoffman, A. C., *Large-Scale Organization in the Food Industries*, TNEC Monograph No. 35, Washington, 1940, pp. 16, 35, 42.

if he could find and protect himself in his own market, he had to turn to it for his credit, his machinery, and his fertilizer, not to mention his clothes and other necessities, including, on a national average, a large part of his food. Not to do so meant to sink to a living standard too low to admit of many of the blessings of democracy. Okies and hillbillies were not the spiritual heirs of Jefferson. The question was, were these farmers-turned-businessmen who operated tractors and milking machines and earned between $600 and $10,000 a year?

Official policy decreed that they were. The very committee that had made the preservation of the family farm a "continuing major objective" of agricultural policy in 1941 fixed lower as well as upper limits for the objective. It resolved that while large farms should be prevented from growing so large as to drive out family farms, small farms should be made large enough to afford a decent living.[21] In 1945, Secretary Anderson declared in his annual report, "The family-sized, owner-operated farm is the backbone of our agriculture and a foundation stone not only of our rural society but of our entire national life."[22]

The family farm is one of the cornerstones of our national land policy. A predominance of family-sized farms redounds to the economic, social and political stability and well-being of the rural community. A predominance of family-sized farms enhances the dignity, productiveness and well-being of a larger proportion of the rural population than would be possible under any other pattern of agricultural land ownership.[23]

The family farm occupied "a high place among ideals in the United States"; it had formed "an integral part of our na-

21. Ezekiel, M., "Schisms in Agricultural Policy," *Journal of Farm Economics*, 1942, Vol. XXIV, pp. 471 ff.
22. *Report of the Secretary of Agriculture*, 1945, p. 150.
23. *Farm Opportunities*, p. 110.

tional farm policy since the days of Thomas Jefferson." [24] The family farm in these official conceptions bore only a theoretical resemblance to the Jeffersonian original.

In one form or another it had been a conscious goal of policy since Jefferson's day. Once an automatic deduction from that "immensity of land" upon which both Locke and Jefferson had based their social ideals, it was at stake now in circumstances comparable to those which the British had met with the enclosure movement and free trade and the French had postponed with the agrarian laws of the Revolution. The immensity of land was gone; the dice were no longer loaded in its favor. It was at issue now in the contentious realm of political theory.

It had never been wholly lost to that realm. As we have seen, Jefferson's original interest in agriculture was political and social rather than economic. The earliest specific measures by which this interest was converted into national policy were the public land laws. These laws applied to the nation the principles Jefferson had applied to Virginia. One by one the states that had not already done so abolished primogeniture and entail. The Land Ordinance of 1785, which determined the whole course of public land policy, and for which Jefferson himself supplied the preliminary draft,[25] enabled the American people to take possession of the public domain in fee simple with no feudal encumbrances, such as quitrents, or other strings attached. As soon as the government had acquired title from the Indians, the land was to be laid out in rectangular townships and sections and sold at auction at a dollar an acre.[26] The price was raised to $2 in 1796, then

24. Jones, R. W., and Goodsell, W. D., *Typical Family-Operated Farms, 1930-45*, Bureau of Agricultural Economics, April, 1946, p. 18.
25. *Works*, Vol. IV, pp. 334-345.
26. Text, Commager, *Documents*, Vol. I, pp. 123-125; Hibbard, B. H., *A History of the Public Land Policies*, New York, 1924,

lowered under the pressure of frontier politicians to $1.25, while the minimum amount of land for sale to individual purchasers was reduced from 640 acres to 80 acres. This meant that a settler could buy a farm for as little as $100.

The whole body of early land laws presents a striking contrast to the contemporaneous British enclosure laws. What the American settlers demanded was free land; and with the Pre-emption Law of 1841 and the Homestead Act of 1862 that is what they got. The Pre-emption Law legalized squatting on unsurveyed public domain, granting the right to purchase claims thus established up to 160 acres at the minimum price after surveyal. The Homestead Act conveyed free title to 160 acres of land to any actual or intended citizen of the United States, over twenty-one years of age and head of a family, for merely residing on, and cultivating, the tract for five years.[27] Future amendments enlarged the size of homestead tracts in wheat- and cattle-raising states to 320, then to 640 acres, and cut the residence requirement to three years (1912). Thus amended, the Homestead Act remained in force until the last of the public domain was withdrawn from private settlement by Presidential order in 1935.[28] Homesteads totaling nearly 250,000,000 acres were patented under its terms, a free gift to the American people of more land than existed within the combined frontiers of Great Britain and France.[29]

The Pre-emption and Homestead laws were neither free of selfish interest in origin nor proof against it in practice.

pp. 61-62; Robbins, Roy M., *Our Landed Heritage*, Princeton, 1942, pp. 7 ff.

27. Text, Commager, *Documents*, Vol. I, p. 410; Hibbard, *op. cit.*, pp. 141-169, and Ch. XVII; Robbins, *op. cit.*, Chs. II, V-VII.

28. Hibbard, *op. cit.*, pp. 392 ff.; Robbins, *op. cit.*, pp. 343-376, 423.

29. The General Land Office count was 247,410,985 acres from 1868 to 1942. *Stat. Abstr., 1946*, p. 162. This was about 390,625 sq. mi. as compared with 301,700 sq. mi., the combined area of Great Britain and France.

The natural desire of the immigrant and the pioneer for free land was opposed from the beginning by eastern landlords and manufacturers, fearful that it would depreciate their real estate values and create a labor shortage in their factories. The issue of free land became entangled with the issue of free soil in the sectional controversy leading to the Civil War. The liberality of the laws favored speculators and monopolists as well as bona fide settlers. Under cover of the Pre-emption Law, which was not repealed until 1891, lumber and mining companies could plant their employees on the public domain and thus acquire large sections of it piecemeal. A commutation clause in the Homestead Act, permitting outright purchase at $1.25 an acre after only six months' residence, played into the hands of land sharks, who advanced the purchase price and (all too often) took the land when it was not repaid. Millions of acres, awarded to veterans as military bounties, found their way into the speculative hopper. Official estimates of grants to railroads from 1850 to 1880 run as high as 187,000,000 acres—an area larger than Texas.[30] So great were these inroads on the public domain that the proportion of new farms started as free patents under the Homestead Act from 1860 to 1900 barely exceeded one-eighth, and the proportion of all farms in tenancy rose to 35 per cent.[31]

30. General Land Office estimate of 1878. The amount was subsequently reduced by forfeiture to 132,458,222 acres by 1942. Cf. Robbins, *op. cit.*, pp. 223 ff.; *Stat. Abstr.*, *1943*, p. 920; Shannon, *Farmer's Last Frontier*, Ch. III.
31. Shannon, *op. cit.*, pp. 55 ff. The tenancy percentage from 1880 to 1940 was as follows:

1880	25.6	1920	38.1
1890	28.4	1930	42.4
1900	35.3	1935	42.1
1910	37.0	1940	38.7

See *Farm Tenancy*, Report of the President's Committee, p. 96; *Stat. Abstr.*, *1946*, p. 596.

All this and worse may be conceded of the land laws without blinking their essential purpose or altogether discrediting their achievement. Their purpose was to make the land available to all comers on equal terms—to distribute it widely among independent landholders in tracts that were for the most part converted into family farms. The purpose was plain in their acreage limitations and residence requirements. It was repeatedly avowed by their supporters. "Tenantry," said Thomas Hart Benton, one of their most energetic champions, "is unfavorable to freedom."

It lays the foundation for separate orders in society, annihilates the love of country, and weakens the spirit of independence. The tenant has, in fact, no country, no hearth, no domestic altar, no household god.

The freeholder, on the contrary, is the national supporter of a free government, and it should be the policy of republics to multiply their freeholders as it is the policy of monarchies to multiply tenants. We are a republic, and we wish to continue so: then multiply the class of freeholders; pass the public lands cheaply and easily into the hands of the people; sell for a reasonable price to those who are able to pay; and give without price to those who are not. I say give without price to those who are not able to pay; and that which is so given I consider as sold for the best of prices . . . a race of virtuous and independent farmers. . . .[32]

Lincoln said he was "in favor of settling the wild lands into small parcels so that every poor man may have a home."[33]

Despite their corruption by sectional, monopolistic, and other selfish interests, these laws represented a conscientious effort to practice the principles of democracy. It is true that without a vast supply of unsettled land at our disposal the laws would not have been possible. It is also true that without the laws an even greater portion of the land might have

32. *Register of Debates in Congress*, 19th Cong., 1st Session, Vol. II, Part 2, pp. 727-728; Hibbard, *op. cit.*, p. 143.
33. Robbins, *op. cit.*, p. 206.

fallen into the possession of speculators and engrossers. Immensity of land did not make Russia a democracy. If it provided the means whereby we translated equal opportunity into economic terms, and if the translation was often faulty and at times almost meaningless, the desire to make the translation accompanied the opportunity. The public land laws were conceived in the Jeffersonian tradition. They kept alive principles in the fat years, when land was plentiful, for reference in the lean years, when it was scarce.

The incorporation of these principles in a formal body of agricultural policy came about slowly and empirically. It began with the founding of the Department of Agriculture and the gradual extension of the latter's activities from the technical and scientific into the economic and social spheres. It was carried to completion by the New Deal. In the process, preserving the family farm slowly evolved from an implicit into an explicit goal of policy, coming to a focus in the Bankhead-Jones Farm Tenant Act and the Farm Security Administration.

The Department of Agriculture was founded in 1862. Its original purpose, as defined by the organic act creating it, was "to acquire and diffuse among the people of the United States useful information on subjects connected with agriculture in the most general and comprehensive sense of that word, and to procure, propagate, and distribute among the people new and valuable seeds and plants. . . ." [34] For this

34. Gaus, John M., and Wolcott, Leon O., *Public Administration and the United States Department of Agriculture*, Chicago, 1940, p. 4. The following account of the evolution of the Department and its policies is based on this and the following works: Shannon, *op. cit.*, Ch. XII; Chew, Arthur, *The Response of Government to Agriculture*, Department of Agriculture, Washington, 1937; Lyon, L. S., Watkins, M. W., and Abramson, V., *Government and Economic Life*, 2 vols., Washington, 1940, Vol. II, pp. 864-948; Blaisdell, Donald C., *Government and Agriculture*, New York, 1940; Department of Agriculture, *Achieving a Balanced Agricul-*

purpose it was granted an initial appropriation of about
$100,000. From these humble beginnings, the Department
was to grow into one of the largest governmental agencies in
the world, with annual expenditures exceeding $1,000,000,000
and public responsibilities touching every phase of our farmers' lives.

It will suffice to mention a few of the outstanding steps in
its progress. The Morrill Act (1862), establishing the land-
grant agricultural colleges, the Hatch Act (1887), providing
federal support for the state agricultural experiment stations,
and the Smith-Lever Act (1914), creating a federal-state
extension service in agricultural education, made it the center
of an educational system that reached from Washington into
the homes of the poorest subsistence farmers. With its Forest
Service and Bureau of Biological Survey, the Department assumed a leading position in the conservation movement. The
Meat Inspection and Food and Drugs Acts (1906) greatly
expanded the powers to regulate trade in agricultural products which it had already assumed prior to their passage. The
next step, from regulation to economic assistance, was taken
with the establishment of twelve Federal Land Banks by
the Federal Farm Loan Act of 1916, which were incorporated
in the Farm Credit Administration in 1933 and placed under
the jurisdiction of the Department in 1939. By this time they
formed but one part of a vast complex of public credit and
insurance agencies, fiscal policies, tariffs, subsidies, and production controls whereby the government participated in the

ture, Washington, 1940; Horton, Donald C., and Shepard, E. F.,
"Federal Aid to Agriculture since World War I," *Agricultural
History*, April, 1945, Vol. XIX, pp. 114-120; Baker, Gladys, *The
County Agent*, Chicago, 1939; Lewis, John D., "Democratic Plan-
ning in Agriculture," *American Political Science Review*, 1941,
Vol. XXXV, pp. 232-250, 454-470; *Abridged List of Federal
Laws Applicable to Agriculture*, USDA, Office of Information,
Document No. 8, July 1, 1946. Specific references below.

direction and management of the agricultural economy—an elaborate, though not necessarily a final, conclusion to a process that started with the collection of seeds.

Not much thought was given to political or economic theory in the early stages of this process, nor was the process wholly agrarian in character. It is true that agrarian groups, particularly the Grangers and the Populists, helped launch the federal government on the career of regulation that began with the Interstate Commerce Act (1887) and the Sherman Anti-Trust Act (1890). But these groups looked to general rather than particular solutions of the farmers' problems. Their first objective was to curb local railroad and warehouse monopolies. Soon they were advocating free silver as a universal panacea; and the Populists stood on a platform containing such planks as a nationally controlled currency, a graduated income tax, postal savings banks, government ownership of railroads, telephone, and telegraph, the secret ballot, woman suffrage, and the direct election of senators.[35] These organizations were called radical in their day. In many respects they were not so radical as the corporate monopolies to which they were opposed, the true embodiments of the new economic and social order. They were trying to enforce through direct legislation the classic democratic principles of individual liberty, equal opportunity, and popular sovereignty. In this they were conservative. Their radicalism consisted largely in their militancy and in their rejection of laissez-faire tactics for a deliberate use of government and public policy as means to their ends. They were only vaguely aware, as the Populists stated in their platform of 1891, that they were participating in a "great social, industrial and eco-

---

35. For origin, aims, and activities of Grange, Populists, and related groups see Buck, S. J., *The Granger Movement*, Cambridge, 1913, and *The Agrarian Crusade*, New Haven, 1921; Hicks, John D., *The Populist Revolt*, Minneapolis, 1931.

nomical revolution now dawning on the civilized world." [36]
The revolution was not just dawning; it had dawned a hundred years ago in England, and the Populists were involved
in it more or less as counterrevolutionists against its organizational forms and social and economic consequences. They
were still a long way from recognizing the true cause of their
troubles or advocating a permanent, special public policy to
alleviate them.

One of the earliest suggestions of such a policy was made
by the Country Life Commission appointed by Theodore
Roosevelt in 1908. Composed of agricultural experts, pro-
gressives and conservationists, among whom Henry Wallace,
Walter Hines Page, and Gifford Pinchot were prominent,
this Commission held hearings throughout the country on
the social and economic conditions of rural life. Its report
(1909) called for "a new and permanent rural civilization
. . . to preserve a race of men in the open country that, in
the future as in the past, will be the stay and strength of the
nation in time of war, and its guiding and controlling spirit
in time of peace." [37] As the chairman of the Commission,
Dean Liberty Hyde Bailey, of the Cornell Agricultural
School, pointed out, the report did not recommend an indis-
criminate back-to-the-land movement but a revival of rural
civilization for those already part of it, to be accomplished
chiefly through religion and education. It would be a "working out of the desire to make rural civilization . . . a world-
motive to even up society as between country and city." [38]
Roosevelt backed up his Commission with a message to Con-

36. Text of platform from Hicks, *op. cit.*, p. 433.
37. Report of the Country Life Commission, Senate Document No.
705, 60th Congress, 2nd Session, 1909, pp. 19-20; Lord, Russell,
The Agrarian Revival, New York, 1939, pp. 52-53.
38. Bailey, L. H., *The Country-Life Movement*, New York, 1911,
pp. 1 ff.

gress urging it to promote "better business and better living on the farm . . . by any . . . legitimate means that will help to make country life more gainful, more attractive, and fuller of opportunities, pleasures, and rewards for the men, women and children of the farms." [39]

The Country Life Movement paved the way for the Smith-Lever Act (1914), co-ordinating the educational work of the Department of Agriculture and the land-grant colleges in a joint extension service. President Taft followed this up by sending to Europe a Commission on Rural Credits and Co-operation, the fruit of whose findings was the Farm Loan Act of 1916.[40] But it was not until the agricultural collapse after the First World War that the whole status of farming as a business and a way of life became a matter of serious public concern. When it did, its importance to society and the body politic was rediscovered and emphatically reaffirmed. Sponsored by the newly organized American Farm Bureau Federation, an "agricultural bloc" organized itself in Congress (1921) under the leadership of twelve senators from western and southern states. As one of them, Senator Capper of Kansas, explained its aims, the bloc recognized "that American welfare depends upon the land and upon a permanent and prosperous agriculture; . . . that national prosperity is dependent primarily upon agricultural prosperity," and that we had "passed into a new era in our national history in which we cannot allow the balance of real production which comes only from the land to get out of balance with the dependent manufacturing industries, commerce, banking and government." The American farm was "the nursery of a genuine freeborn citizenship which is the strength of the

39. Lord, *op. cit.*, p. 53.
40. Capper, Arthur, *The Agricultural Bloc*, New York, 1922, pp. 57 ff.; Lyon, etc., *op. cit.*, p. 877.

Republic," anything which threatened its security "a menace to the national welfare." [41]

The next year, President Harding summoned a National Agricultural Conference, which came to the conclusion that agriculture was a sick industry, affected with sufficient public interest to deserve public assistance. It recommended a "permanent farm policy," including better transportation and credit facilities, but giving prior emphasis to the improvement of individual farm management through co-operation and research.[42] In 1926 the National Industrial Conference Board published the report of an investigation, which declared the position of agriculture to be "of vital concern to all the people of the United States."

> Our farmers are more than a class of our population. Farming is more than an industry. The significance of agriculture in the life of the nation is far deeper than this. It touches something vital and fundamental in the national existence. It involves the national security, the racial character, the economic welfare and the social progress of our people. The development of sound, far-sighted national policies in respect to agriculture is, therefore, one of the most important problems before the country today. Our agriculture is now going through a crucial transition in its character and in its relationship to our national economic life. The success or failure of this readjustment will be of the greatest significance for our future.[43]

The Board then joined with the National Chamber of Commerce in appointing a Business Men's Commission on Agriculture, composed of prominent railroad executives, manufacturers, and bankers, for further study of the question.

41. Capper, *op. cit.*, pp. 3-4. For the organization of the Farm Bureau Federation and its relations with the bloc, see esp. *ibid.* and Kile, O. M., *The Farm Bureau Movement*, New York, 1921; Baker, *County Agent*, pp. 15-24.
42. Cf. Lyon, etc., *op. cit.*, p. 882.
43. National Industrial Conference Board, *The Agricultural Problem in the United States*, quoted in Lyon, etc., *op. cit.*, p. 894.

The opinions of this most un-Jeffersonian body of men possessed a highly Jeffersonian flavor. In their view, the disparity between agricultural and nonagricultural income was not something that could be dealt with "like any other business, industrial or economic question." The farmer's "unique privilege" was "to combine a way of living with the chance for material profit." If he could not make a profit he could not enjoy that way of life. His was "a proud heritage, last bulwark of true democracy," yet the government had neglected it for commerce and industry.

We dare not forget what has been done for financial and industrial development. Why not for agricultural interests?

Agriculture is not merely a way of making money by raising crops; it is not merely an industry or a business; it is essentially a public function or service performed by private individuals for the care and use of the land in the national interest, and farmers in the course of their pursuit of a living and a private profit are the custodians of the basis of the national life. Agriculture is therefore affected with a clear and unquestionable public interest, and its status is a matter of national concern calling for deliberate and farsighted national policies, not only to conserve the natural and human resources involved in it, but to provide for the national security, promote a well-rounded prosperity, and secure social and political stability.[44]

"Husbandry," said the Physiocrats, "is the mother and nurse of other arts. For when husbandry flourishes, all the other arts are in good fettle; but whenever the land is compelled to lie waste, the other arts well-nigh perish." [45] "Agriculture," wrote Bernard Baruch in 1921, "is the greatest and fundamentally the most important of our American

44. Business Men's Commission on Agriculture, *The Condition of Agriculture in the United States and Measures for Its Improvement*, New York, 1927, pp. 6, 15-20; Lyon, etc., *op. cit.*, pp. 895-897.
45. Cf. p. 19 above.

industries. The cities are but the branches of the tree of national life, the roots of which go deeply into the land. We all flourish or decline with the farmer." [46] If Jefferson eventually retreated from his extreme agrarianism to make room for commerce and industry, the leaders of American commercial and industrial enterprise now returned the compliment.

The upshot of all these parleyings and their political undercurrents was that agriculture was finally accepted as a special national interest requiring a special public policy. Somehow or other the balance between agriculture and the rest of the economy had to be redressed. The ratio of prices received by farmers to those they paid must be brought into "parity." The first means employed to that end was the tariff. A parity price formula was written into the McNary-Haugen tariff bill, but though the bill was twice passed by Congress, it was vetoed each time by President Coolidge.[47] Next the Hoover Administration established the Federal Farm Board (1929) with a revolving fund of $500,000,000 to make price-

46. Quoted by Davis, Joseph S., *On Agricultural Policy, 1926-1938*, Stanford University, 1939, p. 25.
47. 1927 and 1928. The following account of parity and the evolution of New Deal agricultural policy is based on Black, John D., *Parity, Parity, Parity*, Cambridge, 1942; Shepherd, Geoffrey S., *Agricultural Price Control*, Ames, 1945; Schultz, T. W., *Redirecting Farm Policy*, New York, 1943, and *Agriculture in an Unstable Economy*, New York, 1945; Wilcox, Walter W., *The Farmer in the Second World War*, Ames, 1947; Gaus and Wolcott, *op. cit.*; Blaisdell, *op. cit.*; Schmidt, Carl T., *American Farmers in the World Crisis*, New York, 1941; Nourse, Edwin G., Davis, Joseph S., and Black, John D., *Three Years of the Agricultural Adjustment Administration*, Washington, 1937; and miscellaneous publications of the Department of Agriculture, e.g.: *Report of the Secretary of Agriculture*, 1934-1945; *Achieving a Balanced Agriculture*, 1940; *Parity Prices: What They Are and How They Are Calculated*, Washington, June 30, 1942. Particular references below.

stabilizing loans and purchases in cotton and wheat; and with
the Smoot-Hawley tariff (1930) it covered agricultural products with the highest protective duties in history. These
measures were but the preliminaries to an array of New Deal
laws and administrative agencies that made the once-free
enterprise of farming subject to comprehensive government
control and substantially dependent on public financial assistance for its existence.

The avowed purpose of these laws and agencies, as stated
in the act creating the Farm Board, was to place agriculture
"on a basis of equality with other industries." [48] Directly or
indirectly, the new administrative agencies as well as the Department of Agriculture's older bureaus and the fiscal, mone-
tary, and foreign trade programs of the Treasury and State
Departments all served that purpose. On the premise that
"conditions in the basic industry of agriculture have affected
transactions in the agricultural commodities with a national
public interest," the Agricultural Adjustment Act of 1933
declared it

. . . to be the policy of Congress to establish and maintain such
balance between the production and consumption of agricultural
commodities, and such marketing conditions therefor, as will re-
establish prices to farmers at a level that will give agricultural commodities a purchasing power with respect to articles that farmers
buy, equivalent to the purchasing power of agricultural commodities in the base period. [49]

48. Text of preamble from Lyon, etc., *op. cit.*, p. 899.
49. Commager, *Documents*, Vol. II, p. 420. Text from USDA, *Compilation of Soil Conservation and Domestic Allotment Act, as
Amended, Agricultural Adjustment Act of 1938, as Amended*, etc.,
Washington, 1940, p. 17. This original legal definition of parity
was revised by the permanent Agricultural Adjustment Act of 1938
to read as follows:
"(1) 'Parity,' as applied to prices for any agricultural commodity,
shall be that price for the commodity which will give to the commodity a purchasing power with respect to articles that farmers

The base period prescribed for all commodities covered by the law, except tobacco, was August, 1909, to July, 1914, for tobacco, 1919 to 1929, the years when these commodities had brought their highest peacetime prices relative to nonagricultural commodities.

As Secretary Wallace and his successors interpreted it, this legislation looked to higher things than prices and income: to the conservation of natural and human resources on a grand scale—soil, housing, health, education, an improved national diet, the co-ordination of supply and demand through an "ever-normal granary"—as well as a larger share in the national income for agriculture.[50] Nor did they overlook the family farm. They recognized it as the "central point" in our cultural background and claimed the AAA would afford it protection "from the competition of large-scale farm operations."[51] As the program developed, however, it was increas-

buy equivalent to the purchasing power of such commodity in the base period; and, in the case of all commodities for which the base period is the period August 1909 to July 1914, which will also reflect current interest payments per acre on farm real estate, and freight rates, as contrasted with such interest payments, tax payments, and freight rates during the base period. . . .

"(2) 'Parity,' as applied to income shall be that per capita net income of individuals on farms from farming operations that bears to the per capita net income of individuals not on farms the same relation as prevailed during the period from August, 1909, to July, 1914."

50. These views are set forth in the annual reports of the Secretary of Agriculture from 1933 to 1945. Cf. also, Wallace, Henry A., *New Frontiers*, New York, 1934, and "Agricultural Security," Address before the American Farm Bureau Federation, Pasadena, December 9, 1936; Nourse, Davis and Black, *Three Years of the AAA*, pp. 561-573; USDA, "Farmers in a Changing World," *1940 Yearbook of Agriculture, passim*; USDA, *Agricultural Policy, 1945*.

51. USDA, *Agricultural Adjustment, 1938-39*, a Report of the Activities Carried on by the Agricultural Adjustment Administration, July 1, 1938, Through June 30, 1939, Washington, G.P.O., 1939, p. 4.

ingly dominated by the concept of parity, and parity was defined almost exclusively in terms of the price of farm commodities instead of the annual income of farmers.[52] The tactics of the farm bloc in Congress and the agrarian political
organizations that prompted it resolved themselves into a
wholesale raising of farm prices to the highest possible level.

To this end the government employed two principal devices. On the one hand, it tried to reduce the supply of basic
farm commodities (a) by curtailing crop acreages, and (b)
by buying the commodities, or taking them as collateral for
non-recourse loans, and holding them off the market in an
ever-normal granary. On the other hand, it padded the
market price of the commodities with subsidies. Through the
powers invested in it by the Agricultural Adjustment Act of
1933, the Soil Conservation and Domestic Allotment Act of
1936, and the Agricultural Adjustment Act that made it a
permanent part of the Department of Agriculture in 1938,
the AAA fixed nation-wide production and marketing quotas
for such basic products as cotton, wheat, corn, tobacco, rice,
milk and its derivatives, cattle, potatoes, peanuts, and others.
County committees translated these quotas into acreage allotments and production quotas for the individual farmers in
each county, and compliance with the quotas was rewarded
with benefit payments from the federal government. When
the Supreme Court, in the Hoosac Mills Case of 1936, ruled
this an unconstitutional control of production, the practice was
resumed and intensified on the principles of conservation and

52. The working formula for determining the parity price of a commodity was to multiply its base period price by the current index
   of prices paid by farmers. If the latter stood at 200, for example,
   and the market price of wheat were 88.4 cents a bushel, the parity
   price would be $\frac{88.4 \times 200}{100} = 176.8$ cents a bushel. Cf. Shepherd,
   op. cit., p. 230. Parity price schedules are published each month
   by the Department of Agriculture in *The Agricultural Situation*.

Congressional regulation of interstate commerce, both of which the Court found constitutional.[53]

The Soil Conservation Act provided for the remuneration of farmers for abiding by "their equitable share, as determined by the Secretary, of the normal national production of any commodity or commodities required for domestic consumption and exports," [54] as well as for shifting from soil-depleting to soil-building crops and other conservation practices; while the permanent Act of 1938 further strengthened the AAA with compulsory marketing quotas, enforceable with tax penalties.[55] It also provided for direct parity payments (in addition to conservation payments) to the producers of the great surplus crops, cotton, wheat, corn, tobacco, and rice. The combined payments, which were scaled upward in amounts lower than $200 and limited to an individual maximum of $10,000,[56] kept most farmers in line—by inducement rather than coercion. By 1942, 6,000,000 of them, representing 85 per cent of the cropland to which the law applied, were on the federal payroll.[57]

The crop reduction program was significant chiefly for these payments. Aggregating $5,500,000,000 from 1933 to 1943,[58] they brought the farmers' cash income that much

53. In Mulford v. Smith, 307 U.S. 38, 1939; Swisher, Carl B., *American Constitutional Development*, Boston, 1943, pp. 902-905, 962-968. The Court ruled out the first AAA because of a processing tax, which it held was a control of production and as such unconstitutional. The succeeding Acts also controlled production, but in the name of conservation and as an exercise of the commerce power, and the Court approved.

54. Text of act from USDA, *Compilation*, p. 5.

55. These could be applied, provided not more than one-third of its producers objected to any of five basic crops, viz., cotton, wheat, corn, tobacco, and rice. *Ibid.*, pp. 27, 32, 39, 45, 49.

56. Statistics and texts of laws from USDA, *Agricultural Adjustment, 1937-38*, Washington, G.P.O., 1939, esp. pp. 19, 309.

57. *Agricultural Statistics, 1944*, pp. 504-505.

58. *Ibid.*, p. 503.

nearer to parity. The program also resulted in substantial gains to conservation. But it failed of its primary objective: it did not reduce the supply of farm commodities. Farmers pocketed their checks for taking part of their land out of cultivation and grew more on what they cultivated. Although by 1942 the acreage of cotton, wheat, corn, and tobacco had been reduced 21 per cent (45,000,000 acres), production of all save cotton, even in the face of some unusually severe droughts, had increased.[59] Forcing the price up by acreage reduction proved a failure.

Parity prices were more directly supported by crop loans and purchases by the Commodity Credit Corporation. These were made at various percentages of the parity price of each commodity fixed by Congressional legislation. Limited at first to cotton, wheat, corn, and a few other crops, they were eventually extended to 166 commodities [60] and by 1945 aggregated $12,000,000,000. Three-quarters of this sum represented wartime purchases, designed to stimulate rather than restrict production; but the whole sum was none the less an investment in parity. Never, even in the grimmest days of the war, did the farm bloc permit Congress to overlook this goal. In 1941 and 1942 it secured the enactment of laws fixing commodity credit loan rates at 90 per cent of parity (92.5% for cotton), the rates to prevail for two years after the first January following the close of hostilities. In 1942 it wrote a clause into the Emergency Price Control Act prohibiting the OPA from imposing a price ceiling lower than 110 per cent of parity [61] on any farm commodity. Thereafter, numerous agricultural price floors rose higher than

59. USDA figures from Schultz, *op. cit.*, pp. 171-173.
60. By the Agricultural Marketing Agreement Act and amendments thereto in 1941 and 1942. Shepherd, *op. cit.*, pp. 54 n., 265-267; Schultz, *op. cit.*, pp. 175 ff.; *Agr. Statistics* '44, pp. 488-490.
61. Or the October or November 1941 market price, whichever was highest. Text of law from USDA, *Parity Prices*.

ceilings, the consumer paying the ceiling price, and the government making up the difference to the producer in subsidies.[62]

These price increases and subsidies were strongly opposed by the OPA, the President, and the wartime public opinion mobilized behind them.[63] They drew from the President one of the strongest public rebukes he ever administered. " 'Parity,' " he said,[64] "is a standard for the maintenance of good farm prices."

It was established as our national policy in 1933. It means that the farmers and the city worker are on the same relative ratio with each other in purchasing power as they were during a period some thirty years ago—at a time when the farmer had a satisfactory purchasing power. One hundred per cent parity, therefore, has been accepted by farmers as the fair standard for their prices.

Last January, however, the Congress passed a law forbidding ceilings on farm prices below one hundred and ten per cent of parity on some commodities. On other commodities the ceiling was even higher, so that the average possible ceiling is now about one hundred and sixteen per cent of parity for agricultural products as a whole.

This act of favoritism for one particular group in the community increased the cost of food to everybody—not only to the workers in the city or in the munitions plants, and their families, but also to the families of the farmers themselves.

There is no better evidence of the political coming-of-age of American agriculture. In ten short years it had developed from a ward of charity into a political force capable of pur-

---

62. Shepherd, *op. cit.*, pp. 264-267.
63. Cf. Senate, 77th Congress, 1st Session, Committee on Agriculture and Forestry, Hearing on Senate Resolution 117, *Formula for Determining Parity Prices*, May 29, 1941, and same, Part 2, July 16-December 19, 1941, Washington, G.P.O., 1941; Black, *Parity, Parity, Parity*, Chs. IV, XVIII; McCune, Wesley, *The Farm Bloc*, New York, 1943, Ch. IV.
64. In a fireside chat on September 7, 1942. Text from Zevin, B. D., ed., *Nothing to Fear*, New York, 1946, pp. 333-341.

suing its own interests even to the point of defying the head of the nation in wartime. After the war, the pendulum continued to swing in the same direction. In fact, it swung so far that instead of committees of businessmen calling on the nation to do something for agriculture, committees in the Department of Agriculture and the Association of Land-Grant Colleges were reminding farmers of their stake in business. Agricultural prosperity "should follow or be concurrent with, rather than precede" industrial prosperity.[65] The "economic well-being of farmers is inseparable from that of the Nation as a whole."

When unemployment rose to almost 14 million people in 1932 and 1933, net income of persons on farms dropped to less than 3 billion dollars—the lowest level since farm income records were begun in 1910. When unemployment fell to less than a million people in 1943 and 1944, net farm income climbed to 14 billion dollars—an all-time high. . . .[66]

High-level employment in non-agricultural industry means very much more to farmers than any "farm program" the government may attempt.[67]

These admonitions were more than mere reflections of the full-employment philosophy that dominated British and American economic thought at the close of the era. In source and tone as well as in content, they were signs that the campaign for agricultural equality, begun in earnest in 1933, had not only reached, but might even have overshot, its mark.

Economists have presented a formidable case against the parity program.[68] The keynote of their thinking is full pro-

65. *Farm Opportunities*, p. 4.
66. *Report of the Secretary of Agriculture*, 1945, p. 82.
67. *Postwar Agricultural Policy*, Report of the Committee on Postwar Agricultural Policy of the Association of Land-Grant Colleges and Universities, October, 1944, p. 8. Cf. *Agricultural Policy*, USDA Miscellaneous Publication No. 589, Washington, 1945, p. 38.
68. See esp. Schultz, *Agriculture in an Unstable Economy*, and Shepherd, *Agricultural Price Control*, *passim*.

duction and employment in the whole economy, not production curbs to raise prices in any part of it. As they see it, the fundamental cause of the farm problem is too many farmers, too many people trying to make a living in agriculture relative to the comparatively inflexible demand for agricultural commodities and the constantly improving techniques for producing them. From this basic maladjustment ensue all the others: the underemployment of agricultural labor shown up so vividly by the war,[69] the price-depressing surpluses, the low income, and the correspondingly inferior cultural opportunities. The fundamental solution to the problem was to transfer labor from agriculture to industry. To effect the transfer, industrial jobs were necessary; to create the jobs, full industrial production. Agricultural prices that led backward to a demand situation that not only no longer existed but was not even expected to recur were not a comprehensive or a permanent policy for agriculture but the guarantee of a *status quo* in which all its basic maladjustments were frozen. The first criterion of the economists is waste. They sharply criticized an agricultural program the effect of which was to restrict the rate of national economic progress by keeping farm prices high, by providing the nation with its food at more than minimal labor costs, and by obstructing the flow of labor from farming to relatively more productive industrial employment.

Official opinion was not oblivious to this criticism. As the program unfolded, Secretaries Wallace, Wickard, and Anderson advocated progressively broader and more permanent goals than parity prices. Wallace emphasized the storage operations of the CCC, designed to stabilize prices with relation to both production and demand and maintain an ever-

69. See the symposium on farm tenure entitled *Family Farm Policy,* J. Ackerman and M. Harris, eds., Chicago, 1947, esp. Chs. II, III, XVI-XIX and XX.

normal granary, soil conservation, security of farm tenure, and an improved national diet, objectives for which he thought "security for agriculture" a more fitting slogan than "equality." [70] In his last year in office, a Departmental pamphlet entitled, *Achieving a Balanced Agriculture*, summed them up as "security, conservation, abundance and stability"; [71] and a post-war publication, over the signature of Secretary Anderson, as "adequate farm and forest production, parity of income for farmers, efficient production and distribution of farm products, parity of services and facilities (schools, roads, hospitals, housing, electricity, etc.), for rural people, and good tenure conditions, with special emphasis on the family farm." [72] Secretary Wickard's committee specifically recognized the contradiction between the objectives of economically profitable family farming and keeping the greatest possible number of people in farming.[73] And in 1941 the Chief of the Bureau of Agricultural Economics, Howard R. Tolley, conceded that although parity income was "a more rational and equitable approach" than parity prices, the latter formula was "generally accepted among a surprising number of people—among them farmers, consumers, administrative officials of the government, and legislators . . . an advantage that cannot be brushed aside." [74] It is plain from these statements that prices had dominated policy and politics prices. All the same, they were agrarian politics, and victorious: that, to us, is their great significance.

70. Cf. his speech to the American Farm Board Federation, Pasadena, Dec. 9, 1936, entitled "Agricultural Security," quoted in Nourse, etc., pp. 561-573.
71. *Op. cit.*, 1940, p. 21.
72. USDA, *Agricultural Policy*, 1945, pp. 4-5.
73. Ezekiel, M., "Schisms in Agricultural Policy," *loc. cit.*
74. Tolley, H. R., "Agriculture and the Parity Yardstick," Address before the National Co-operative Milk Producers' Federation, Chicago, Nov. 11, 1941. Text from Shepherd, *op. cit.*, pp. 321 ff.

When Franklin D. Roosevelt called for the first parity legislation he termed it "a new and untrod path." [75] It was neither. The Pharaohs of Egypt had trodden it, the Chinese, the Greeks and Romans.[76] Public regulation of the supply and price of food was new among the principal nations only to the United States. Even in the United States its newness consisted in putting an old principle into practice. Agriculture had long been credited with a public interest transcending the production of food. What more logical corollary to this principle could there be than that the public should contribute to the support of agriculture beyond and above the price of food? The parity price policy was the main form in which this contribution was made.

The second most important part of the New Deal's agricultural policy was its farm credit program. When it came into power, the Roosevelt Administration found on its hands a farm population on the verge of bankruptcy. In 1929 its mortgage indebtedness had reached a total of $9,750,000,000, about 12 per cent of which was held by the government and the rest by private institutions. The ensuing depression precipitated a tidal wave of foreclosures. The value of farm property went down so fast that by 1935 mortgage debts on full owner-operated farms had passed 50 per cent of the total value of those farms.[77]

To meet these conditions, the Federal Land Banks and

75. "I tell you frankly that it is a new and untrod path, but I tell you with equal frankness that an unprecedented condition calls for the trial of new means to rescue agriculture." Roosevelt, Franklin D., *The Public Papers and Addresses of*, New York, 1938, Vol. II, p. 74.

76. Cf. Lacy, Mary G., "Food Control During Forty-six Centuries," address before the Agricultural History Society, Washington, D. C., March 10, 1922; quoted by Shepherd, *op. cit.*, pp. 17-19.

77. *Agricultural Statistics, 1944*, p. 459; *1940 Yearbook of Agriculture*, pp. 742-745.

Intermediate Credit Banks, created respectively in 1916 and 1923, were co-ordinated with two new sets of lending agencies, namely the Federal Production Credit Corporations and the Federal Banks for Co-operatives, under the general direction of the Farm Credit Administration. The four agencies were established in twelve regional offices, analogous to the Federal Reserve districts, and their resources made available to individual farmers, agricultural credit institutions, and co-operatives. With funds provided by the Federal Farm Mortgage Corporation, the Land Banks undertook the refinancing of farm mortgages on a scale that helped reduce their total to $6,500,000,000 by 1940 and at the same time increased the government's stake in that total from 12 to 40 per cent.[78] While mortgages constituted their main business, the various FCA banks also made short-term emergency-crop and drought-relief loans, supplied working capital both to production associations and co-operatives and to individual farmers, and in general afforded more diversified and flexible credit than could be obtained from private sources.

From 1934 to 1940, loans outstanding from these banks averaged over $3,000,000,000 a year.[79] The infusion of this public credit saved thousands of farmers from disaster, and with them, their social institutions and the way of life they represented. FCA loans to production credit associations, particularly, were a boon to small-scale farmers. But, as one

---

78. *Agricultural Statistics, 1944*, pp. 459, 473. Details of farm credit system from Schmidt, *op. cit.*, Ch. VI; Gee, *op. cit.*, Ch. X; *1940 Yearbook*, pp. 740-754. Cf. also Benedict, Murray R., "The Relation of Public to Private Lending Agencies (in Agriculture) and Recent Trends in Their Development," *Journal of Farm Economics*, 1945, Vol. XXVII, pp. 88-103; Black, John D., "Agricultural Credit Policy in the United States, 1945," *Ibid.*, pp. 591-614.

79. *Agr. Statistics, 1944*, p. 459.

of its governors put it, the FCA slogan was credit, not charity.[80] It had to protect its own financial position, and to do so it was obliged by law to maintain collateral requirements beyond the means of the farmers whose need for public assistance was greatest.[81] Neither the FCA nor the AAA, nor both together, could repair the social structure of American agriculture at its weakest point. With their credit requirements and their emphasis on price, both tended to benefit farmers who produced for the market more than they did those who produced primarily or exclusively for their own consumption.[82] The latter, particularly the tenants and dispossessed owners, whose numbers swelled the statistics of

80. Schmidt, *op. cit.*, p. 215.
81. Long-term (5-40 year) Federal Land Bank Mortgages, for example, were limited to 50% of the appraised normal value of the land plus 20% of the appraised value of the permanent insured improvements upon it. They were obtainable through national farm loan associations, in which the mortgagee was required to subscribe for stock equal to 5% of the amount of the mortgage. The association then subscribed for the same amount of Land Bank stock, to an aggregate of not more than $50,000. Short-term Land Bank Commissioner loans secured by second mortgages and limited to $7,500 could also be obtained at a slightly higher rate of interest. Nearly three-quarters of the FCA's total loans outstanding were comprised of these two types of mortgage. Cf. *1940 Yearbook*, pp. 749 ff.; House of Representatives, 79th Cong., 2nd Sess., *Hearings before the Subcommitte of the Committee on Appropriations, Agriculture Department Appropriation Bill for 1947*, pp. 1078 ff. The Frazier-Lemke Act passed in 1934, invalidated by the Supreme Court and again passed in revised form in 1935 also brought relief to farmers in the form of mortgage and bankruptcy moratorium procedures. See "A Permanent Bankruptcy Chapter for Farmers," 56 *Yale Law Journal*, 982-1016.
82. See in this respect the testimony of Secretary Wallace in House of Representatives, 75th Cong., 1st Sess., 1937, *Hearing before the Committee on Agriculture on H.R. 8*, A Bill to Establish the Farmers' Home Corporation and to Encourage and Promote the Ownership of Farm Homes, etc., p. 360; H.R., 78th Cong., 2nd Sess., *Report of the Select Committee to Investigate the Activities*

debt and distress reported by the President's Committee on Farm Tenancy, had to look elsewhere for assistance—assistance that would have to spring primarily from social ideals rather than from economic expediency.

This they found in the third part of the New Deal's agricultural policy, the part featured by the Farm Security Administration. With this agency the New Deal revived the Jeffersonian ideal and made the family farm an explicit goal of policy. Originating with the rural relief work of the Federal Emergency Relief Administration and the Division of Subsistence Homesteads in the Department of the Interior, in 1933, the Farm Security Administration began its career in 1935 as the Resettlement Administration.[83] The RA made rehabilitation loans to farmers too poor to obtain credit elsewhere, purchased submarginal farmland and retired it from cultivation, resettled families, thus displaced, in model farm communities, and built "green belt" suburban towns on the outskirts of Washington, Cincinnati, and Milwaukee as demonstrations of land use and city planning.[84] Incorporated in

of the Farm Security Administration, House Report No. 1430, p. 86. Schultz, op. cit., pp. 168 ff., 211, and others criticize AAA parity payments as "regressive."

83. History and Activities of FSA from H.R., 78th Cong., 1st Sess., Hearings before the Select Committee of the House Committee on Agriculture to Investigate the Activities of the Farm Security Administration, Parts 1-4, May 11, 1943-May 3, 1944, esp. Part 3, "History of Farm Security Administration and Its Predecessors"; same committee, 78th Cong., 2nd Sess., Report (House Report No. 1430); Farm Security Administration, Reports of the Administrator, 1938-1945; Schmidt, op. cit., Ch. VII; Gaus and Wolcott, op. cit., pp. 240 ff.; Alexander, W. W., "Overcrowded Farms," 1940 Yearbook, pp. 870-886. USDA, Toward Farm Security, Washington, G.P.O., 1941, and Farm Security Administration, Washington, G.P.O., 1941. Particular references below.

84. Resettlement Administration, Report of the Administrator, 1937, pp. 16-18.

the Department of Agriculture on January 1, 1937, the agency's repertoire was expanded by the Bankhead-Jones Act of the following summer to include farm purchase loans to tenants and dispossessed owners, and on September 1, it was rechristened the Farm Security Administration. As such it continued till August 14, 1946, when it was again reorganized and rechristened the Farmers' Home Administration.[85]

The FSA operated on the same organizational pattern as the Farm Credit Administration, with twelve regional offices, and local facilities in most of the nation's agricultural counties. In addition to the duties inherited from the Resettlement Administration and enjoined on it by the Bankhead-Jones Act, it built and maintained the farm labor camps that sheltered the Okies in John Steinbeck's *Grapes of Wrath*, gave its clients technical assistance with their crops and livestock, taught them methods of conservation, helped them form co-operatives, and provided them with medical care. Though its activities sometimes overlapped those of the FCA, its sphere was legally, and for the most part practically, distinct. Local committees had to certify that its clients were too poor to obtain assistance from the FCA or any other source and, further, that they were worthy of assistance, before their applications for loans could be accepted. Once the loan was made, moreover, FSA agents supervised its use, advising the borrower as to how best to apply it to his own particular farm and household.

If the FCA's slogan was credit, not charity, the FSA's was social rehabilitation, not credit. It was this fundamentally sociological, noneconomic purpose that gave it distinction. It represented a decision not to let economic and technological trends run their course, as the British had done, but to resist

85. By the Farmers' Home Administration Act of 1946, Public Law No. 731, 79th Cong., 2nd Sess.

them in defense of the agrarian way of life and the family farm. With the passing of the Bankhead-Jones Act, this decision was confirmed in both law and political philosophy. Testifying in favor of the act, Secretary Wallace, who had served as chairman of the Committee on Farm Tenancy that had recommended it, declared the aim of the act to be that of "saving rural America from the absentee owner and the landless farmer."

Our homestead and reclamation movements were aimed primarily at putting the agricultural land of the Nation into the hands of owner-operators. The family-sized farm, owned by the man who operated it, was the ideal of our past land-settlement policy. But we failed to safeguard the ownership of the land which was homesteaded to such an extent that a large proportion of our best farm land fell into the hands of speculators and absentee landlords. Today we are faced with the problem of stemming the tide of tenancy, and reconstructing our agriculture in a fundamental manner by promoting farm ownership among the tillers of the soil. In this manner we can give our Nation greater social and political stability, while at the same time we are promoting individual opportunity and security.[86]

The main purpose of the bill was proclaimed in its title: "to encourage and promote the ownership of farm homes and to make the possession of such homes more secure."[87] In 1943 the Administrator of the FSA acknowledged under the cross-questioning of a House investigating committee "one central purpose—fostering property ownership by family-type farmers and thereby preserving and strengthening the traditionally American family-type of farm operation."

Our rehabilitation borrowers are family-type operators. Our efforts with them have all been in the direction of strengthening their hold on their farms by fostering property ownership among

86. House, *Hearing on H.R. 8*, pp. 357-358.
87. *Ibid.*, p. 1.

them. . . . Our tenant purchase borrowers are all owners of family-type farms. Loans are made to them for the purpose of making them owners of their farms.[88]

Ironically, this statement was made in defense against charges of tampering with the institutions of private property and the family farm, so serious that they had led to a Congressional investigation of the FSA. In support of his position, the Administrator could show that its rehabilitation and tenant purchase programs absorbed 98 per cent of its funds and affected 99 per cent of the families it had aided.[89] But in the early years of the Agency, its administrators, and some of their colleagues in the Department of Agriculture, had been assailed by what one of their most sympathetic critics calls "a flicker of doubt"[90] as to the future of the family farm in the American economy. The first administrator of the Resettlement Administration, Rexford G. Tugwell, had misgivings with regard to fee-simple ownership, which he thought too often overburdened the farmer with debt and forced him into tenancy.[91] Others, including Secre-

88. Statement of C. B. Baldwin, FSA Administrator, House Investigating Committee *Hearings*, pp. 5-6.

89. *Ibid.*, p. 5. As of June 30, 1945, the FSA reported rehabilitation loans totaling $921,418,558 and representing approximately 860,000 borrowers since 1935, and 38,089 farm ownership loans totaling $228,336,146 since 1938. See *Annual Report, 1944-45*, pp. 13-14.

90. Eaton, Joseph W., *Exploring Tomorrow's Agriculture*, New York, 1943, p. 80. Although incomplete and avowedly sympathetic to them, this is the only systematic study of the co-operative corporation farms of the FSA. It must be supplemented with the reports and hearings cited above and following.

91. *Investigating Committee Hearings*, pp. 42 ff. Tugwell was Administrator of the RA in 1935. He was succeeded by W. W. Alexander (Acting Administrator of the RA 1935-1937, Administrator of FSA 1937-1940), C. B. Baldwin (1940-1943), Frank Hancock (1943-1946), and Dillard B. Lasseter (1946-   ).

tary Wallace, Undersecretary M. L. Wilson, FSA Administrator C. B. Baldwin, and various members of the President's Committee on Farm Tenancy, were sufficiently impressed with the impetus technology was giving to large-scale farming to favor experimenting with it.[92] The President's Committee, though advocating as a general policy the "establishment of family-size farms," suggested the initiation of co-operative farming and land tenure "on an experimental scale." [93]

Accordingly, while the FSA devoted its main energies to strengthening the foundations of the privately owned family farm, it also supported a few large-scale farms of a different character. In 1940 it had under its management 164 rural community projects of varying types, 8 of which were of its own creation and the rest inherited from the Resettlement Administration.[94] The great majority of the projects consisted of groups of small, individually leased and operated family farms on government-owned tracts of land. About 15 of them, on the other hand, were organized as "cooperative corporation farms." These farms, which in 1943 numbered 13, with a total membership of approximately 300 families,

92. *Ibid.*, pp. 21 ff., 42 ff., 55-59; Eaton, *op. cit.*, Chs. VI, X; Senate, 78th Cong., 1st Sess., *Hearings on Agricultural Appropriation Bill for 1944*, p. 625.

93. "In some cases cooperative groups may well be aided to acquire land by purchase or long lease for subleasing to group members. The cooperative organization would serve the function of a non-profit-seeking landlord, working in the interest of its membership. Such an arrangement would relieve Federal agencies of much responsibility for management. It is recommended that such a policy be initiated also on an experimental scale." *Farm Tenancy*, p. 13. Cf. Investigating Committee, *Report*, pp. 12, 78.

94. FSA, *Annual Report, 1940*, pp. 13-14; Senate, 78th Cong., 1st Sess., *Hearings on Agricultural Appropriation Bill for 1944*, p. 630.

were managed and operated as large-scale units.[95] Through directors and managers chosen from their own membership, their members employed themselves at wages roughly corresponding to the wages for farm labor prevailing in the vicinity. At the end of each fiscal year, they shared in the net earnings of the farm (if there were any) in proportion to the number of hours of labor each had contributed. Each member was furnished with his own house and a small garden plot on which he could raise vegetables and keep a few livestock. A few of the co-operatives allowed their members an acre or two apiece from which they could supplement their income with truck crops. Members were free to leave at will, receiving cash settlements for their equities when they did so; and the only requirements for admission—besides observance of the various state laws governing co-operatives—were that candidates must be low-income farmers and receive the approval of the farms' directors.[96]

In addition to this departure from the principle of independent family farming, the FSA made an experimental departure from the principle of fee-simple ownership. It granted 10 community farms the use of their land on 99-year leases, and 1 on a 40-year lease. Among the 11 were 3 of the co-operative corporation farms just described. The rest were simply co-operative associations which subleased their land in

95. Because of inconsistencies in both terminology and procedure, the exact number of these farms is difficult to determine. Eaton, *op. cit.*, pp. 65 ff., says there were 27 in March, 1942, but the number officially reported to Congress that year was 15, on 4 of which "nearly all" and on the remaining 11 "only a portion" of the land was operated co-operatively. See House, 77th Cong., 2nd Sess., *Hearings on Agriculture Department Appropriation Bill for 1943*, Part 2, pp. 253-257. Cf. *idem*, 1944, pp. 1034-1036. By 1943, when the FSA came under investigation, the number had declined to 13. Investigating Committee, *Hearings*, pp. 19-21.

96. Investigating Committee *Hearings*, p. 1005; Eaton, *op. cit.*, Chs. VII-XV.

conventional family units for individual occupancy and operation.[97]

The co-operative farms and the 99-year leases were attempts to improve the position of the small-scale, low-income farmer in the industrial age. The co-operative was intended to make available to him the technological and economic advantages of large-scale corporate farming, the 99-year lease, to obviate the difficulties of capital accumulation incidental to fee-simple ownership. The co-operatives were also defended as "one of the most effective methods of rehabilitating and reclaiming the low-income farm families . . . especially those who have been down-and-outers for many generations," [98] of training them for the eventual responsibilities of family farming, and, incidentally, of enabling them to contribute to the war effort.[99] But their advocates saw them chiefly as "a possibility of adjustment for farmers to the requirements of the 'agricultural revolution' without sacrifice of the economic democracy hitherto enjoyed by some of them"—potential "pilot plants of a new pattern of land ownership, land use and social organization." [100] In the words of Secretary Wickard, they were "an attempt to find a means of enabling the small farmer to join with other small farmers and to approach the efficiency of large undertakings so that the advantage of large purchases and large sales and better machinery" could be obtained; ". . . an experiment to determine if there are ways for the small farmer to meet the

97. Investigating Committee *Hearings*, pp. 15-20, 1004-1006.
98. Senate, 77th Cong., 2nd Sess., *Hearings on Agricultural Appropriation Bill for 1943*, p. 655.
99. *Ibid.*, pp. 653-664.
100. Eaton, *op. cit.*, pp. 81-86. Cf. testimony of C. B. Baldwin and Secretary Wickard, House, 77th Cong., 2nd Sess., *Hearings on Agriculture Department Appropriation Bill for 1943*, pp. 256 ff., 740 ff., and C. B. Baldwin, H. Gordon and R. W. Hudgens in Investigating Committee *Hearings*, esp. pp. 25 ff., 505 ff.

terrific competition you have with the big tractors and all that sort of thing." [101]

It was these farms and leases more than anything else that led to the Congressional investigation of the FSA. The argument before the Congressional committees, upon which both sides knew the fate of the experiments, and indeed of the entire agency, depended, was mainly ideological. According to the prosecution, the purpose of the FSA, as defined by the Bankhead-Jones Act, was to stimulate "individual ownership, with a view to promoting individual ambition and industry." The co-operative farms represented "if not the reverse, the converse let us say, of that proposition . . . the policy of collective farming, called cooperative farming." [102] Members of these farms had no chance to exercise the right of fee-simple ownership. They shared expenses and profits in common. They labored in common. The only discernible difference between this and "communistic farming in Russia is that under the Farm Security Administration plan the participation in the projects is of a voluntary character whereas in Russia such participation is compulsory." [103] Since this was "in direct conflict with the intent of Congress and with the ancient land policy of this Nation," [104] the projects should be abolished.

The co-operative farms and 99-year leases were not the only activities of the FSA to come under attack, nor were these the only charges levied against them. But they were the ones that received the greatest emphasis. When the Administrator of the FSA pointed in defense to the minor role they played in the agency's total program, the Chairman of the Investigating Committee replied, "This is a small part of

101. House, *Hearings on 1943 Appropriation*, pp. 740-741.
102. *Ibid.*, pp. 255-256.
103. *Ibid.*, p. 740.
104. Investigating Committee *Hearings*, p. 2.

your activities, but it is very important because it involves a great principle; it goes deep into the traditional land policy of this country." [105]

With that principle and that policy the Administrator protested complete agreement. He endorsed the Bankhead-Jones Act. He agreed with the Investigating Committee that fee-simple ownership was "deep in the traditions of this country"; he did not think anything else was "acceptable to our farm families." [106] In fact, as the investigation proceeded, none of the FSA's officials or its supporters had much more to offer for the co-operatives and the 99-year leases than apologies. Secretary Wickard had already testified after a visit to one of the most prosperous of the co-operatives that its members "still tend toward individual ownership." [107] The FSA Administrator, himself a champion of the co-operatives, was even more emphatic on the point:

I know, from our experience in operating resettlement projects, that the thing that most of our farm people want, the poor people of this country, the people who have been denied, for many reasons, the privilege of owning property—I know that the thing they want beyond anything else is to get security through property ownership. When I say "property ownership," I mean the ownership of livestock, tools and equipment, and ownership of land. [108]

When a regional director of the FSA was asked why he took people so far "down the scale" on one particularly unproductive co-operative, he explained it was because "these 28 families that we got last year were the only ones that we could get, and we scoured all of eastern North Carolina to get them." The explanation was accepted as proof "that even though those families might be poor people they are still

105. *Ibid.*, p. 21.
106. *Ibid.*, p. 21.
107. House, *Hearings on 1943 Appropriation*, p. 747.
108. Investigating Committee *Hearings*, p. 44.

Americans and believe in the policies of America, and don't want to go on into a collective matter . . . that the American people won't go for that stuff." [109] Finally, in response to charges of financial extravagance in this and other activities, the Administrator admitted that the most successful of all the co-operatives was operating at a loss that would probably amount to 25 per cent of the capital investment, and that no co-operatives had yet been developed "that wouldn't require some subsidy out of the Federal Treasury." [110]

Fortified with this evidence, the Investigating Committee brought in a report (May 9, 1944) calling for liquidation of the co-operatives and the 99-year leases and an expansion of the tenant-purchase program. It condemned the "co-operative or communal farm projects" as "dismal failures," "a farce and a fizzle," and as evidence that the FSA "has been used as an experiment station of un-American ideas and economic and social theories of little or questionable value." [111] The "clear intent" of the Bankhead-Jones Act was "to encourage individual farm-home ownership and to aid and assist in the rehabilitation of the destitute farm families on individual family-size farms. . . ." [112] The FSA had defied the will of Congress. Through its co-operative farms and similar projects it "apparently owned and controlled more acreage of cultivated land than any other public or private agency in the Nation." It had become "the Nation's largest landlord" and was "conducting farming operations on a larger scale than any other individual or corporate farm owner in America." [113] The Committee did not consider it necessary "to discuss the virtues or merits of the fee-simple ownership

109. *Ibid.*, p. 522.
110. Senate, 78th Cong., 1st Sess., *Hearings on 1944 Appropriation*, p. 626.
111. House Report No. 1430, pp. 12, 13, 23.
112. *Ibid.*, p. 5.
113. *Ibid.*, p. 5.

of property as compared with the policy of the 99-year leases and collective farming enterprises, further than to observe that the courts of all American jurisdictions look with favor upon the vesting of fee-simple title and the experiments referred to are incompatible with the land policies which Americans have cherished throughout the years." [114] The experiments must be abandoned, the full resources of the FSA concentrated on increasing "the trend of ownership of family-sized farms." [115]

The mandate of the Investigating Committee was carried out. The Chairman of the Committee followed up its report with a bill whose first two objectives were listed as "prompt liquidation of Government interest in cooperative farming and landholding projects" and "no more 99-year leases in the farm-security program." [116] On August 14, 1946, the bill became a law. It abolished the FSA, preserving only the credit facilities in its program of tenant-purchase and rehabilitation loans. These it merged with the similar facilities of the Emergency Crop and Feed Loan Division of the Farm Credit Administration in a new agency known as the Farmers' Home Administration. The latter was empowered (1) to make loans to farm tenants to enable them "to acquire, repair or improve family-size farms," (2) to insure mortgages designed for the same purpose, and (3) to make production and subsistence loans up to $3,500 for five years at 5 per cent. As in the past, clients had to satisfy local committees of their inability to obtain credit from other sources, and the entire act rested on two significant provisions: The first prohibited any loan "for the carrying on of any land-purchase or land-leasing program, or for the purpose of carrying on operations in collective farming, or co-operative

114. *Ibid.*, p. 17.
115. *Ibid.*, p. 25.
116. House Report No. 1747, 78th Cong., 2nd Sess., p. 2.

farming." [117] The second stipulated that no loan should be made or mortgage insured "for the acquisition, improvement, or enlargement of any farm unless it is of such size and type as the Secretary determines to be sufficient to constitute an efficient family-type farm-management unit." [118]

Thus ended the "flicker of doubt," if not in people's minds, at least in public law and policy. Notwithstanding the sanction it had long since given to the co-operative principle in the purchase, sale, and even processing of farm commodities,[119] Congress had frowned upon its application to the tenure and use of land. It did nothing to disturb private corporate farms; on the contrary, it conferred on them their full share of parity and conservation payments. But it decreed that when it came to setting a public example, the example should be set with the small, independent family farm held in fee-simple ownership. Thus it completed the definition of a policy that had begun with farmers in general and ended with farmers in particular, that in the beginning had taken the family farm for granted and in the end had made it a specific item of national interest. On this high level it was incorporated in President Truman's Economic Report of 1947.

The cycle of policy thus concluded sets the United States apart from both England and France. It shows a national concern for agriculture as a state of society, for private prop-

---

117. Short Title [amendment to Title IV of the Bankhead-Jones Farm Tenant Act]. Sec. 44(a) (4), Public Law, 731, p. 8.

118. *Ibid.*, Title I, Sec. 1(c), p. 13.

119. In the Capper-Volstead Act of 1922, which provided that "persons engaged in the production of agricultural products as farmers, planters, ranchmen, dairymen, nut or fruit growers may act together in associations, corporate or otherwise, with or without capital stock, in collectively processing, preparing for market, handling, and marketing in interstate and foreign commerce, such products of persons so engaged." Cf. Gee, *Social Economics of Agriculture*, pp. 351 ff.

erty in land, and for family farming as their mainstay, that has simply not existed in England—a concern that played little part in the development of British democracy and almost throttled its development in France. It is impossible, obviously, to interpret the differences between the three countries, in this or any other respect, solely in terms of political theory. Our greater wealth of land and natural resources has enabled us to do things that neither of the others could do, to industrialize like the British and protect the agricultural *status quo* like the French, to avoid *parcellement*, and so on: the list of practical qualifications and conditions could be extended indefinitely. Still, there is enough theoretical identity among the three to suggest the limits within which our political theory of family farming may be carried out in practice. The British experience shows us that it is possible to reduce the farm population to an irreducible minimum, and small, owner-operated family-size farms virtually to extinction, and still have democracy. The French contrast shows us that it is possible to maintain a maximum farm population and carry family farming to its extreme logical conclusion, and all but lose democracy in the bargain.

In the most recent phases of our public policy for agriculture, we have been fumbling and groping for a mean between these two extremes. On paper the policy contemplates the best of two worlds: the economic efficiency of the British, and the individual enterprise of the French; an agricultural population, proportionately larger than the British, settled on independent, economically profitable family farms that would be counted large-scale commercial ventures in France. In practice it promises everything to everybody: parity to corporation as well as family farmers, subsidies all round, the worst of two worlds as well as the best. The Second World War and the world-wide demand for American farm products that followed it have put a gloss of prosperity over these confusions and contradictions. But no one—least of all the farmers themselves—expects it to last. When it wears off we shall again be confronted with the need of a constructive, truly national, long-range agricultural policy. What will its guiding principles be? Out of the confusions and contradictions of the past ten years, one central purpose has crystallized—in theory. We have resolved to achieve an optimum farm population whose characteristic unit of production is an efficient family-size farm. Whether the resolution can be made effective remains to be seen.

CHAPTER SIX

Prospects

W<small>HAT ARE</small> the prospects for the policy we have just reviewed? Are the dominant political forces in American
agriculture behind it? Is it so full of the common sense of
our time that we can expect it to prevail whether they are
momentarily in favor of it or not? Like all political theory,
the one we are considering is a bridge between past, present,
and future, a bridge that is never completed but is always in
process of construction. For the process to keep pace with the
course of events, it must constantly discover new foundations
to supplement, often to replace, the old.

Our theory originated partly as the rationalization of our
economic environment, partly as an ancient tradition, and
partly as a fortuitous relationship between both and a war for
independence that turned into a democratic revolution. It is
no more possible to base exclusive agrarian claims to democracy on our present-day economic environment than it is to
assume the universal possession of farm land or universal
employment in agriculture. The axiomatic equation of Jefferson's day is no longer a valid basis of public policy. To
make it such is to imply that most Americans are beyond the
democratic pale and that their only means of redemption
would be a back-to-the-land movement and a reduction of
the total population and the national standard of living that
not even Jefferson, to judge him by his practical afterthoughts
on the subject, would approve. This much is evident from
the census figures.

The same is true of the ancient tradition according to which
agriculture is the most exalted (and as Jefferson projected

the tradition, the most democratic) occupation, and its corollary, that the size of the farm population is the best measure of a nation's welfare and its democracy. These ideas appealed to Jefferson and his colleagues in a day when the political circumstances of a republican revolution seemed to bear them out. They cannot be proved to have been true in the first place, and they certainly cannot be proved true today. Millions of Americans who have found careers outside of agriculture deny them. The migration of farmers and their children to cities, in search of such careers, and the plight of many who stay behind disprove them. They do not stand up well in the face of a rural standard of living that has been thoroughly and vividly documented:[1] 1,500,000 farms—a quarter of the total—with incomes of $600 or less in 1945; 52 per cent of our farm families with incomes of less than $1,000 in 1935 and 1936; a rural malnutrition rate (though farmers are supposed to eat well) twice as high as the urban; a rate of draft rejections for physical disability of 54.4 per cent among farmers and farm managers and 52.8 per cent among farm laborers—the third highest rate in the country;[2] two-thirds of our farm families inadequately housed—a third in rural slums "in houses so poor that they are virtually be-

1. See especially Gee, Wilson, *The Social Economics of Agriculture*; Brunner, E. deS., and Kolb, J. H., *A Study of Rural Society* (3rd ed.), New York, 1946; USDA, *Toward Farm Security*, Washington, 1941; Taylor, Carl C., Wheeler, Helen W., and Kirkpatrick, E. L., *Disadvantaged Classes in American Agriculture*, USDA, Washington, 1938; Schwartz, Harry, *Seasonal Farm Labor in the United States*, New York, 1945; Goldschmidt, Walter, *As They Sow*, New York, 1947; also, for health statistics, U.S. Selective Service System, *Medical Statistics Bulletin No. 3*, November 1, 1944, and for general economic and population statistics, 1945 Census of Agriculture.

2. This was the rate among white farmers only, which was exceeded only by the rate among domestic servants, unemployed, and relief workers. With Negro farmers included, it was second to none. *Selective Service Bulletin No. 3*; Brunner and Kolb, p. 575.

yond repair"; [3] the nation's highest birth and infant mortality rate; 65 per cent of the rural population without access to public libraries; 10,000,000 rural children dependent on educational facilities which the New York *Times* in its recent survey [4] of the nation's educational system described as "tragic"; the most fertile source of the country's population, with its most wretched economic and cultural opportunities.

Individual farmers may still find in agriculture the most morally and esthetically rewarding way of life; individual writers may still find their pleasant valleys; but the only reasonable conclusion to draw from the facts is the one the British Royal Commission drew from its study of English rural conditions in 1924: that the appreciation of rural life that mattered was the appreciation of farmers, not writers, that in all countries large numbers of farmers "express that appreciation by the rural exodus," and that how ideal rural life is "is a matter of opinion on which they have had something to say." [5] "The idealization of rural living is one of the stumbling blocks to understanding life as it is in America," two of the most ardent contemporary champions of family farming have written. "You can't escape the modern world by retreating into farming." [6] If there were democratic magic in agriculture, why is it that men have been farmers for thousands of years, yet democracy as we know it is not two hundred years old and claims a minority of the earth's peoples as its disciples? That the democracy of which Aristotle said the best material was an agricultural popula-

---

3. *Report of the Secretary of Agriculture*, 1946, p. 76. Cf. *The Agricultural Situation*, April, 1947, p. 3.
4. Including the worst buildings, the poorest, most inexperienced, and worst-paid teachers, and a teacher shortage. New York *Times*, February 19, 1947.
5. Cf. above, pp. 84-85.
6. Waring, P. Alston, and Golden, Clinton S., *Soil and Steel*, New York, 1947, p. 25.

tion would not be recognized as such today, Aristotle himself makes all too clear. For he goes on to explain that its citizens would be too poor and too hard-working to trouble themselves with public affairs, and so patient and long-suffering that they would even endure tyrannies "as they still endure oligarchies, if they are allowed to work and are not deprived of their property." [7] The truth of the last part of his statement, so palpable a contradiction of the first part, has been borne out over and over again. Farmers have been called the backbone of every form of government in the world, including fascism and communism. Democracy did not flourish in England until the political power of the agrarian aristocracy had been broken and British agriculture had been deliberately discounted as a way of life. To the extent that it can be said to have flourished in France, it did so in spite of the agrarian community rather than because of it. Whatever truth the proposition may have held in the United States of Jefferson's age, it has lost a little of it with each succeeding generation. Beginning with the Jackson Administration, the "mobs of great cities" have made ever-increasing contributions to democracy, in educational processes and philosophy no less than in politics. If democracy suffered its worst American perversion in boss rule through city machines, it has also derived much of its essential humanitarianism and still more of its intellectual freedom from the communal life of towns and cities. And while city-dwellers have supported corrupt bosses, they have also supported the most liberal national leaders and spokesmen of democracy in recent years.

Democracy did not spring full-flowered from the soil. It has grown from men's minds and spirits, in the commercial and industrial atmosphere of cities as much as—some would

7. Aristotle, *Politics* (Jowett Translation), VI, par. 4.

say more than—in the agrarian atmosphere of the country. "Democracy, where it appeared, was a phenomenon of the city . . . ," a distinguished contemporary critic writes of its earliest phases in Greece and Rome. "The city (*polis*) was the state, the rest of the country was its hinterland, the territory it owned. Democracy was the prerogative of citizens— and citizens were still city-dwellers." [8] Towns and villages played a dominant role in its later development in Europe; British democracy was city-bred; even in eighteenth-century America, where cities in the modern sense did not exist and towns of any size were few and far between, who would deny the creative influence of the New England town meetings, of Revolutionary Boston and Philadelphia?

Today, with the rural community protesting the superior cultural advantages of the urban, the conception of democracy as an agrarian phenomenon is less valid than ever. The statistics do not lie. They are vouched for by Congressional investigations as well as by the human documents of Steinbeck, McWilliams, Walter Goldschmidt, and others. Evidence taken by the House of Representatives Select Committee to Investigate the Interstate Migration of Destitute Citizens (1941) and National Defense Migration (1941-42), which fills thirty-three volumes, and by the Senate Committee on Education and Labor (1940-42), builds up into a picture of agrarian distress, insecurity, and social inequality hardly matched in western Europe. Half a million sharecroppers in a state of feudalism; half a million migratory workers roaming the highways; another half million farm families scratching for subsistence on submarginal soil: [9] these

8. MacIver, R. A., *The Web of Government*, New York, 1947, p. 179.
9. Taylor, Wheeler and Kirkpatrick, *Disadvantaged Classes*, p. 58; House of Representatives, 80th Cong., 1st Sess., *Hearings before the Committee on Agriculture on Long-Range Agricultural Policy*, April-May, 1947, Part I, pp. 9-70.

are members of our agrarian society. This is not to reproach
the poor with their poverty. The famous colloquy between
one of Steinbeck's Okies and a tractor driver whom he has
threatened to shoot for knocking over his buildings and
plowing up his land shows the direction, if not the precise
location, in which the blame lies:

"It's not me. There's nothing I can do. I'll lose my job if I
don't do it. And look—suppose you kill me? They'll just hang
you, but long before you're hung there'll be another guy on the
tractor, and he'll bump the house down. You're not killing the
right guy."

"That's so," the tenant said. "Who gave you orders? I'll go
after him. He's the one to kill."

"You're wrong. He got his orders from the bank. The bank
told him, 'Clear those people out or it's your job.'"

"Well, there's a president of the bank. There's a board of directors. I'll fill up the magazine of the rifle and go into the bank."

The driver said, "Fellow was telling me the bank gets orders
from the East. The orders were, 'Make the land show profit or
we'll close you up.'"

"But where does it stop? Who can we shoot . . . ?" [10]

The Okie could not shoot the industrial revolution. He could
not shoot our failure to devise a public policy that would put
that revolution to the advantage of our whole population.
But he could, and did, testify to the fact that, in his case, and
the cases of a million or more of his fellows, agriculture by
itself had performed no democratic miracles.

Whether our contemporary agrarian society is more democratic than any other in its political aims and organizations
is likewise a matter of opinion. Farmers support both major
parties and are found on both sides of most major political
issues. In an age in which economic representation has become
an extraconstitutional feature of government, and in circum-

10. *The Grapes of Wrath*, The Viking Press, Inc., New York, 1939,
pp. 51-52.

stances in which, as we have seen, agriculture was already overrepresented constitutionally, they have organized according to their economic interests, like everybody else. Their main distinction in this respect is that whereas business and labor have organized and brought pressure to bear on government largely from the outside, farmers have done so from within as well as from without.

We have observed the main steps that took them into government and the government into farming. The Production and Marketing Administration illustrates the latest results of these trends. In 1946, in a general reorganization of the Department of Agriculture, the Agricultural Adjustment Administration, the Commodity Credit Corporation, and twelve other offices were incorporated in this new agency. The manifold activities of the Department were now grouped in three basic divisions: (1) the Agricultural Research Administration, which includes the Department's basic research bureaus, such as Animal Industry, Plant Industry, Soils, and Agricultural Engineering; (2) the Production and Marketing Administration, embracing its "action" programs; and (3) its miscellaneous independent agencies with highly specialized functions, notably the Soil Conservation Service, Farm Credit Administration, Farmers Home Administration, Rural Electrification Administration, Bureau of Agricultural Economics, and Office of Foreign Agricultural Relations.[11]

The whole vast complex amounts to one of the most far-reaching and subtle combinations of public and private enterprise in the world. The PMA is divided into ten commodity branches,[12] each of which is responsible for planning and

11. See *Report of the Administrator of the Production and Marketing Administration*, 1946.
12. Cotton, dairy, fats and oils, fruit and vegetable, grain, livestock, poultry, special commodities, sugar, and tobacco.

"encouraging achievement" of production goals for its commodity. Its means of encouragement are adjustment subsidies, price subsidies, marketing quotas, import and export programs, and similar devices; and each is assisted by a functional branch and field service. The goal for a given commodity is first determined by its PMA commodity branch in consultation with representatives of state and local committees. Next it is submitted to the approval of state Department of Agriculture Councils and of the Secretary of Agriculture. Thence it goes to state PMA committees, appointed by the Secretary of Agriculture, and from these to elective county and local community committees—known as agricultural conservation committees—who "carry it down the road," as the saying goes, to the individual farmer.[13] To this basic pattern, with differences in detail, the Soil Conservation Service, the Farmers Home Administration, and, in the counties in which it exists, the Rural Electrification Administration all conform. It is an amalgam of federal, state, and local government, in which farmers participate as farmers rather than as ordinary citizens, in which they share directly in the formulation and execution of public policy in agriculture at every level from Washington to the grass roots.

The system has been subject to the same controversy that has raged around every other recent projection of federal initiative into heretofore private enterprise and state and local government. It has been criticized both as radical government regimentation and as the reactionary machination of agricultural big business. It is hard to find evidence of an undemocratic design on the part of the government. On the contrary, when local initiative seemed threatened by centralization, Secretary Wallace, M. L. Wilson, Milton Eisenhower, and other officials in the Department of Agriculture

13. PMA, *Report of Administrator*, 1946, pp. 1-18.

took steps to protect it. They negotiated an agreement between the Department, representing the federal government,
and the land-grant colleges and universities, representing the
states and local communities (the Mt. Weather Agreement,
July 8, 1938), according to which the traditional relations
between the federal government and the states in research
and education were to be preserved, while all planning in
connection with the new action programs was to begin in
local communities with local committees. Community plans
were to be co-ordinated for counties by county committees;
county plans for states, by state committees; and state plans
in a national land-use planning program, by the Department
of Agriculture. Community planning committees were to
consist entirely of local farmers; state and federal officials
were to be represented on all others. Eisenhower thought the
Mt. Weather Agreement "should go far to justify faith in
the efficacy of democratic methods in dealing with great national problems." [14] So it did, until the war suspended its
operation. It went even farther to prove the good faith of
the federal government. In an age in which the governments
of the world have been steadily extending their powers over
the economic life of nations, it was remarkable evidence of
respect for the fundamental democratic principles of individual freedom and local self-government.

The charge that the whole system has been unduly influenced by agricultural big business is more difficult to answer.
We have noted the fact that notwithstanding its sliding scale
of payments and its upper limit of $10,000, the parity price
program obviously benefited the top third of our farmers,

14. Eisenhower, Milton S., and Kimmel, Roy I., "Old and New in
    Agricultural Organization," *1940 Yearbook*, p. 1135. See also
    "Cooperative Land Use Planning—A New Development in De-
    mocracy," *ibid.*, pp. 1138-1156; Lewis, John D., "Democratic
    Planning in Agriculture," *loc. cit.*; Lord, Russell, *The Wallaces of
    Iowa*, Boston, 1947, pp. 380-382.

who produce for the market, more than it did the bottom third, who have little or nothing to sell; and we have also seen that notwithstanding the social philosophy of Wallace and his colleagues, the price program came to dominate the whole policy of which it was a part. It is the judgment of students of the Land Use Planning Committees created under the terms of the Mt. Weather Agreement that they were more representative of "leading farmers" than they were of the rank and file, and that the whole experience "has shown very clearly that it is difficult to make vocational representation much more extensively representative than the traditional type of territorial representation." [15] Spokesmen for the lower ranks of agrarian society have been of the same opinion regarding the whole New Deal system. "We note with interest and hope recent speeches of Secretary Wallace in which he states that the Department of Agriculture has heretofore throughout its history been concerned primarily with the top third of the farmers in the country and that it must turn its attention to the others from now on," the representative of the Southern Tenant Farmers' Union on the President's Committee on Farm Tenancy declared in his minority report in 1937. "But our experience has been such that we cannot believe the Department of Agriculture will be able in any near future to remove itself from domination by the rich and large landowning class of farmers and their political-pressure lobbies. The county agricultural agent . . . is a symbol of such domination." [16]

What are these "political-pressure lobbies" and what do they stand for? There are three national organizations that represent the interests of farmers in general, the National

15. Lewis, *op. cit.*, p. 468; cf. Baker, *County Agent*, Ch. IV, esp. pp. 100-101.
16. *Farm Tenancy*, p. 21.

Grange, the Farmers' Educational and Co-operative Union of America, and the American Farm Bureau Federation.[17] The oldest of these is the Grange, founded in 1867 and reporting a dues-paying individual adult membership of 746,000.[18] The next oldest is the Farmers' Union, founded in 1902 and claiming an individual membership of 400,000.[19] The youngest is the Farm Bureau Federation, founded in 1920, with a family membership of 1,128,259.[20] These are supplemented by the National Council of Farmer Co-operatives, with a membership of 109 co-operative associations, representing 5,000 local co-operatives, with more than 2,000,000 members,[21] and by a large number of specialized producers' associations, among the most important of which are the National Co-operative Milk Producers' Federation, the National Livestock Marketing Association, the American Sugar Cane League, and the National Wool Growers' Association.

One and all maintain nation-wide organizations that keep watch over legislation and administrative policy in Wash-

17. Background and details of farm organizations from Baker, *County Agent*; Wing, DeW. C., "Trends in National Farm Organizations," USDA *1940 Yearbook*, pp. 941-979; Blaisdell, D. C., *Economic Power and Political Pressures*, TNEC Monograph No. 26, Washington, 1943; McCune, Wesley, *The Farm Bloc*, New York, 1943; Kile, O. M., *The Farm Bureau Movement*; "The Farm Bureau," *Fortune*, June, 1944, Vol. XXIX, pp. 156 ff.; the annual reports, resolutions, and official publications of the three organizations, esp. the American Farm Bureau Federation's *The Nation's Agriculture* and *Official News Letter*, and the Farmers' Union's *National Union Farmer*; and Congressional Hearings cited in Chapter Five and below.

18. As of June 30, 1946. Goss, A. S., Master (to author), Oct. 1, 1946.

19. Statement of James G. Patton, president, who claimed "more than 400,000 members." *Hearings on Long-Range Agricultural Policy*, April 29, 1947, p. 132.

20. AFBF *Annual Report*, 1946, p. 13.

21. National Council of Farmer Co-operatives, *Blue Book*, *1947*, p. 14.

ington and the state capitals. It goes without saying that each consults the special interests of its members, and the narrower those interests, the narrower its counsels of public policy. In this respect each conforms with a trend which the Temporary National Economic Committee summed up as follows:

Because of the concentration of economic power in the organizations which dominate commerce and industry, we have found individuals forming new national organizations to deal with new problems. First are the national trade associations established and maintained by dealers and manufacturers in many lines. Commercial organizations have become regional and even national. Farmers have their national farm organizations to protect their interests in the field of national business. Finally, organized labor, which was first purely local and then became a national federation of local unions, produced a wholly national organization which was designed to cover the same areas covered by big business and big Government. From the leaders of all of these organizations in their central offices go out to individual members all over the country the suggestions which direct their group activity. Frequently, instead of the organization being directed by the thought and will of its members, the action of members is directed by the thought and will of the leaders. This has necessarily followed because one result of the development of centralism is that individuals are no longer in contact with information which is essential to the formation of policy vital to their existence.[22]

Of the aims of the three general—hence most representative—organizations, the agricultural policy reviewed in the previous chapter is a composite. All three endorsed the original Agricultural Adjustment Act of 1933. Time and again since then each has gone on record before Congress and the public in favor of parity, soil conservation, the AAA, the Commodity Credit Corporation, and the general principles and scheme of public policy for agriculture these repre-

22. TNEC, *Final Report and Recommendations*, 77th Cong., 1st Sess., Senate Document No. 35, March 31, 1941, p. 10.

sent.[23] All three have recently testified in favor of its continuation. At a joint conference in early April, 1947, the Farm Bureau Federation, the Grange, and the National Council of Farmer Co-operatives lined up behind it with practical unanimity, while the Farmers' Union, which stood aloof and advocated changes of emphasis so great as to approximate changes of principle, also accepted its basic provisions.

This is brought out clearly in the testimony of the leaders of the three organizations to the House of Representatives Committee on Agriculture in the Hearings on Long Range Agricultural Policy it conducted later in the spring.[24] Speaking for the conferees, the president of the Farm Bureau Federation said that, as a result of the basic legislation enacted since 1933, it could now "properly be said that this Nation, for the first time in its history, has had a definite national policy for agriculture. Since nearly all of the laws have been passed with bi-partisan support, I believe we are justified in saying that the farm issue has been taken out of politics. I fervently hope that this situation may continue. . . . My first plea to you gentlemen and to Congress—and I make it with great earnestness—is this: Please don't destroy our farm program." [25] The president of the Union admitted, under pointed questioning, that he would not scrap any major part of it.[26] The Grange, true to its tradition, showed itself to be more protectionist than the other two organizations, the Union, more disposed to co-operate with organized labor. All three wanted decentralized administration of the program, though in different forms. The main difference be-

23. See their annual convention reports and official publications, 1933-1947, also Congressional *Hearings* cited in Chapter Five and below.
24. House, 80th Cong., 1st Sess., Parts 1 and 2, April 22-May 2, 1947, pp. 29-69, 91-175.
25. *Ibid.*, pp. 30-31; cf. pp. 50-58.
26. *Ibid.*, esp. pp. 158 ff.

tween them, the one that came nearest to a difference in principle, was their attitude toward the family farm. All three endorsed it in principle, but whereas this was a pious resolution to the Federation, far down on its agenda and incidental to other things, and the Grange gave it only slightly greater emphasis, to the Farmers' Union it was, and is, almost the be-all and the end-all. The slogan of the Federation and its allies might have been "parity, not charity." The Union presented its program in the form of an act entitled "The National Family Farming Act of 1947," an act which placed "the expansion and prosperity of family-type farming in the United States, with the ultimate goal in view of an agriculture made up of economic size and type family farms" ahead of parity, soil conservation, full production and consumption, and any and all other goals.[27]

The Grange is not the militant organization that it was in its heyday, nor is it anything like as strong as the Farm Bureau Federation. With its membership concentrated largely in the East, and a social program at least as important as its political one, it is proverbially conservative and tends to line up with the Federation on issues of great moment. The membership of the Farmers' Union is even smaller, and also concentrated—for the most part among small farm-owners and tenants in the Midwest. But its militancy and its earnest efforts to put forward a national program rather than a composite of sectional and local interests enhance its stature.[28] The main features of contemporary agrarian politics stand out most clearly in the contrast of its views and actions with those of the Farm Bureau Federation, the most powerful farm organization—some say the most powerful lobby of any kind—in the country.

27. Text of act, *ibid.*, p. 133.
28. Cf. Heald, Morrell, *The Farmers' Union: Threat or Promise,* unpublished ms., Yale University Graduate School, 1947.

The Union, as the avowed champion of the poor family farmer, has pitted itself against the Farm Bureau Federation as the alleged champion of the large-scale commercial producer. According to the Union and its sympathizers, the Federation is the ringleader of an alliance composed of itself, the Grange, the National Council of Farmer Co-operatives, the Co-operative Milk Producers' Federation, and other big producers' organizations representing the "top tier" of farmers, processors, and distributors [29]—"the DuPonts and Girdlers of agriculture, displacing the family farmers just as the giant business corporation displaces the independent small business man." [30] Among the more serious concrete charges they level at the Federation are these: that it exerts an improper influence on the Department of Agriculture through the Extension Service; that it led the fight against the Farm Security Administration, not for the reasons stated in the official testimony but because its southern members were afraid that the FSA's program of tenant rehabilitation would diminish their supply of cheap labor, etc., etc.; [31] and that it attacked the Bureau of Agricultural Economics "as part of its general effort to bring all agricultural policy formulation under its own domination." [32]

These are no partisan canards. The Federation's intimacy with the government through the Extension Service is common knowledge. Secretary Wickard once called it "the closest

29. McWilliams, *Small Farm and Big Farm*, p. 22. Waring and Golden, *op. cit.*, p. 31.
30. Fryer, Lee, *The American Farmer*, New York, 1947, p. 47.
31. Waring, P. Alston, and Teller, W. M., *Roots in the Earth*, New York, 1943, Ch. IX; Lamar, Howard, *The American Farm Bureau Federation*, unpublished ms., Yale University Graduate School, 1947.
32. Hardin, Charles, "The Bureau of Agricultural Economics under Fire: A Study in Valuation Conflicts," *Journal of Farm Economics*, August, 1946, Vol. XXVIII, p. 638.

public-private relationship that exists in agriculture today." [33]
As we have noted, the Extension Service is the system of
adult education and vocational training in agriculture maintained jointly by the federal government and the states. It
originated with the state agricultural colleges and experiment
stations, not long after the passing of the Morrill Act (1862),
and was placed on its present basis by the Smith-Lever Act
in 1914. At the head of the Service is the Director of Extension Work in the Department of Agriculture, who approves
and co-ordinates state projects. These are administered by
Extension Directors in the state agricultural colleges, appointed by the colleges with the approval of the Secretary
of Agriculture. The State Directors employ administrative
assistants and technical specialists, who in turn supervise the
work of the Service's main body, the county agents. [34]

The cost of the Service is borne by the federal government
on the one hand and state and county governments and private
organizations on the other. The federal government con-
tributes $10,000 annually to each state giving legislative
assent to the Smith-Lever Act and beyond that matches the
contributions of the state and its counties dollar for dollar.
Private contributions, officially reported as such, may be included in the county funds. In 1944, contributions from all
four sources amounted to $37,000,000, of which $19,000,000
came from the federal government, $8,500,000 from the
states and state colleges, $8,200,000 from the counties, and
just over $1,000,000, or 2.7 per cent, from private farm or-

33. House, *Hearings on Agricultural Appropriations for 1943*, Part 2,
p. 736.
34. I.e., county agricultural agents. In 1944 these numbered 3,971 out
of a total staff of 9,180, including county agricultural agents and
assistants, home demonstration agents and assistants, rural youth
club agents and specialists. Cf. Brunner, E. deS., Sanders, I. T.,
and Ensminger, D., *Farmers of the World*, New York, 1945, pp.
183-184; *Agricultural Statistics, 1944*, p. 568.

ganizations.[35] Much the largest contributor among the latter was the Farm Bureau Federation, two-thirds of whose contributions were concentrated in Iowa and Illinois.[36] Thus, while most of the Extension Service's personnel is administratively responsible to the states and counties, it is equally dependent on the federal government for its financial support, and in its higher branches equally responsible to it for appointments and general policy; and the Service's chief functionary, the county agent, is at once the servant of the federal government, the state government, the county government, and, to a greater or lesser degree, of the Farm Bureau Federation.

But the latter owes more to the county agent than the contribution it makes to his salary. Department of Agriculture officials have called the county agent "the John the Baptist of the farm bureau movement," and Farm Bureau officials have recognized him as "the keystone of the federation." [37] The Federation's indebtedness to the county agent dates back to the early history of both. The first county agents were technicians, sent out by the Department of Agriculture in 1904 to show southern farmers how to fight the boll weevil. Some of the counties in which these technicians worked found their help so valuable that they hired them as permanent demonstrators. Northern and western counties followed suit with the graduates of agricultural colleges, whom they employed to conduct farm management surveys and demonstrate scientific methods of cultivation. The practice spread, and with the passing of the Smith-Lever Act, these county agents became the principal teaching faculty of our national system of adult agricultural education. Meantime, to help finance and promote their work, farmers had organized into county

35. Brunner, etc., *op. cit.*, p. 183.
36. Baker, *op. cit.*, p. 154.
37. Official testimony quoted by Baker, *op. cit.*, pp. 21-22.

committees, or "farm bureaus," as they came to be called, the first in Binghamton, New York, in 1911.[38] The bureaus spread with the agents, the county bureaus federated in state bureaus, and in 1920 the state bureaus formed the national Farm Bureau Federation.

In this way the Federation gained a much stronger hold over the county agent than is indicated by its 2 per cent share in the financing of the Extension Service. Many states passed laws making the existence of a county farm bureau a prerequisite to the appointment of a county agent and holding him legally responsible to the county bureau thereafter. County farm bureaus still function as county extension associations and administer local extension funds in about twelve states.[39] Even in states in which no legal or financial obligation to do so exists, the relationship between the county farm bureau and the county agent is so old and intimate, and its co-operation so vital to the success of his work, that he defers to it of necessity. When the American Farm Bureau Federation took its fateful step from education into politics, the political importance of this relationship doubled; and when the New Deal added to the educational activities of the Extension Service its vast array of administrative programs, it redoubled. Although their attitude toward these programs was by no means uniformly sympathetic, county agents in general played important roles in them, at least as consultants, at most as organizers and chairmen of their county committees.

This privileged position of a private pressure group with

38. This was organized as a subdivision of the local Chamber of Commerce to reclaim abandoned farms around the city. The first bureau consisting entirely of farmers appears to have been that of Pettis County, Missouri, organized in 1912. Baker, *op. cit.*, p. 12.

39. As reported in correspondence by H. W. Gilbertson, Office of the Director, U.S. Extension Service, to John W. Davidson, Graduate School, Yale University, June 3, 1947.

a foothold in government and an access to public funds explains much of the opposition to the Federation. The fact
that it is defended in law in only a dozen states and that some
of these are in the process of abolishing it gives its critics
little comfort. It holds true without law in many others.
More than that, the Federation would like it to hold true
everywhere. The main complaint of the Federation's president to the House Committee on Agriculture at its long-
range policy hearings was that the system of agricultural
administration built up by the New Deal was not under the
decentralized control of the Extension Service, and his main
suggestion for long-range policy reform was that it be put
there.[40] In the light of the relations between his organization
and the Extension Service in the states and counties, the pro-
posal is not surprising. It may have contemplated, as he said
it did, both economy and a greater degree of self-government
for all concerned. It can hardly have failed to contemplate
a more certain measure of control over all phases of agricultural policy by the Farm Bureau Federation.

This was probably the chief motive, also, of the Federation's attack on the Farm Security Administration. The Federation repeatedly tried to have the FSA abolished, to have
it merged with the Farm Credit Administration, and, failing
these, to whittle down its appropriations and limit its scope
to the strictest letter of the Bankhead-Jones Act.[41] It is true
that the Federation was not wholly united in the matter.
While its Florida, Louisiana, and Arkansas bureaus were telling their members that the FSA was part of a socialist plot
to confiscate their lands, some of its northern bureaus took
neutral stands and even passed resolutions in the FSA's

40. On a grant-in-aid basis, with the federal government matching
    state funds 50-50. *Hearings*, pp. 37-38, 50-58, 68.
41. Cf. Congressional *Hearings* cited in Chapter Five.

favor.[42] Without a doubt the national Federation's opposition reflected the particular fears—and particular influence—of its southern members. Without a doubt it also reflected disapproval of the collectivist aspects of the FSA's co-operative farms that was not confined to any section. The most satisfactory explanation seems to be that the Federation opposed the FSA as "the poor man's extension service," an independent agency over which it had no control, and which therefore represented a challenge to its power and prestige.[43] This is also true of its opposition to the post-war expansion of the powers and activities of the Bureau of Agricultural Economics, particularly in the field of social investigation, a factor in bringing about the resignation of the BAE's chief, and another makeweight for the suspicion that the Federation's main objective is "to bring all agricultural policy formulation and administration under its own domination."[44]

The Federation denies that it is hostile to the small farmer or indifferent to his interests. It claims to be "the most democratic organization in the world,"[45] fully representative of all sections and farmers. The Iowa Farm Bureau, second only to the Illinois in size, and second to none in importance, sets forth its political philosophy as follows:

Ours is a pressure group organization, developed to carry the volunteer opinions and actions of farm people through their own free, independent, unfettered general organization to their county,

42. Moore, Arthur, "Earl Smith: Farmers' Boss," *Atlantic Monthly*, January, 1945, Vol. CLXXV, p. 90; Lamar, *op. cit.*, pp. 23 ff.; *Iowa Yearbook of Agriculture, 1946*, p. 309; Davidson, John W., *The American Farm Bureau Federation and the Iowa Farm Bureau Federation*, unpublished ms., Yale University Graduate School, 1947, p. 19.

43. Cf. Lamar, *op. cit.*, p. 23.

44. Hardin, *op. cit.*, pp. 638, 666-667.

45. *Hearings on Long-Range Policy*, p. 50.

state and national governments. A member of the Farm Bureau is a volunteer member, not a result of a check-off system. Some of our farm people take our democracy for granted. We believe the founders of our government planned and anticipated for group organization; otherwise they would have provided for a narrow form of government that did not allow pressure groups. They had experienced narrow forms of governments with kings, emperors and czars. They chose a form of government that could swing to the extreme left or to the extreme right, dependent upon the will of the people to bring it back through a representative form of government. The Board of Directors of the Iowa Farm Bureau symbolizes our democracy at work through group action.[46]

The Federation may claim to represent the needy as well as the prosperous, but it has not won their allegiance, and the reason it has not done so is obvious. Its members are not "callous to the troubles of the poor," writes a sympathetic midwestern critic who thinks the Federation's corn belt bureaus are truly representative. "They simply do not consider the Farm Bureau to be a welfare agency." [47] The Federation stands for agriculture as a business, not as a way of life, and it fights for the greatest possible share for that business in the nation's income. Who shares the share, in what proportions, and with what consequences to democracy, is not its primary concern. It speaks the language of business and politics. Its business is parity prices; its politics are well described in *Official News Letter* cartoons ridiculing "one man alone individualism" in a game of "powerful organized groups competing for economic advantage." [48]

It has learned to play that game so effectively that many observers of the national scene consider it the most powerful

46. *Iowa Yearbook of Agriculture, 1941*, pp. 419-420. Quoted by Davidson, *op. cit.*, p. 17.
47. Moore, Arthur, "Earl Smith: Farmers' Boss," *loc. cit.*, p. 90.
48. October 3, 1945. Cf. *ibid.*, August 7, 1945, February 20, 1945, January 23, 1946.

lobby in Washington. But as the stakes of the game are prices, production controls, and marketing quotas, and as nearly half of our farmers produce so little that they do not have enough to eat, much less to sell, they do not qualify as participants. The president of the Farmers' Union has explained why they are not members of the Farm Bureau Federation:

The consequences of poverty—disease, ignorance, early death—still take a terrible, unaccountable toll among the 3,000,000 farm families who market but 10 per cent of the commercially sold farm products. And many thousands of others sell but little more. . . .

From the standpoint of parity of income or fair exchange value for agriculture as a whole, then, it becomes clear that we must do something about these more than 3,000,000 farm families. It will never be possible to bring farm income up to its fair share of the national income simply by raising prices of farm products. Even granting that consumers would continue to buy at the prices that would be necessary, which is doubtful, so long as half of all farm families obtain only 10 per cent of the benefit of those prices, then it is clear that the total of farm income will forever remain below that proportion of the national income that it should attain. Every dollar of every price boost gives roughly 90 cents to those farmers who are better off and 10 cents to those who need increased income. The result is that the children and the land that are the long-time victims of rural poverty become progressively more disadvantaged. While agricultural prices obviously must be protected, it is just as obvious that something more needs to be done.[49]

It was that "something more" that the Farmers' Union proposed in its "Family Farming Act of 1947." The main purpose of the act, as it was expounded by the Union's president, was "a new approach to a general agricultural program, an approach dedicated to making the family-type the predominant unit of American agriculture."

49. *Hearings on Long-Range Policy*, p. 145.

Every major agricultural measure in the past has attempted to solve farm problems by tinkering with price mechanisms. While we recognize the importance of a fair price and fair exchange value for farm commodities, we submit that the history of all this legislation shows that it has been only partially successful. We still believe in the price and income parity concepts, although we do not believe that they should be so rigidly applied as they have been in the past. We do not want to throw overboard any of the hard-won gains of agriculture in the past decades.

But we want to go further, to move ahead to something new. . . . Congress and farm organizations have proclaimed over and over again their allegiance to the family farm ideal. They are well justified. The family farm pattern is the healthiest pattern for agriculture, from every standpoint. "American agriculture," the Colmer committee has said, "throughout its development was characterized by individual family-sized owner-operated farms. This contributed greatly to the independent spirit and moral character of the entire population, and was the backbone of our political and economic democracy as they developed in America."

Upon the family farms grow independent, strong, alert citizens. The family farm is the final stronghold against oppression, whether economic or political, and no tyranny or "ism" will ever thrive in a country that grounds its agriculture on that base.

Family farming is just as efficient as factory farming. It has been losing out in competition because of the cheap migratory labor available to the latter. Unprotected by minimum wage or other laws, "rootless and homeless," this labor has shared less in the fruits of its toil than any other group in America. "Remove this reservoir of cheap labor—in effect a subsidy at the expense of humanity—and it is doubtful if family farming would suffer in the comparison of efficiency." Under existing circumstances, the family farm, "that economic unit upon which our democracy was based in the beginning," is disappearing. Only aggressive action can save it. "That is why, in this presentation and in proposing a draft bill, we have centered our attention on those steps that must be taken to enable family farms to compete successfully with bigger farms and in a generally industrialized economy." [50]

To this end the "Family Farming Act" would decentralize our whole system of agricultural administration; only instead of placing it under the Extension Service, it would put it in the hands of county committees of farmers and agricultural laborers, "freely elected under safeguards similar to those contained in the National Labor Relations Act." [51] These committees would be guided by a National Farm Price and Production Committee, also elective, composed of twenty-two farmers (two from each of the country's major agricultural regions), which would determine production goals and prices in consultation with a Consumer Protection Agency. To improve the condition of agricultural labor and in this respect equalize the terms of competition between family and factory farmers, the Minimum Wage Law and the Fair Labor Standards Act of 1938 would be extended to agriculture. A Conservation Works Program with an annual budget of $500,000,000 would employ farmers and farm laborers who could not find full-time employment on farms. Every farm family with one working farmer would be guaranteed a minimum cash income of $1,000. The Farmers' Home Administration would undertake "the purchase of farming units of greater magnitude than are susceptible of single-family operation, the survey and subdivision of such units into economic family-type units . . . and the resale of such economic family-type units to qualified purchasers . . . also . . . a program of purchase and resale of land to the end that farming units too small for economic family-type operation may be enlarged to economic size"; [52] and the whole program would be supported by a general policy of

50. Testimony of James G. Patton, President, National Farmers' Union, *Hearings on Long-Range Policy*, pp. 145-147.
51. *Ibid.*, p. 147.
52. Title III, Sec. 301(a), *ibid.*, p. 138.

full employment and production, subsidized consumption, dietary improvements, and foreign trade designed to expand the agricultural market to a maximum.

Here was a plan for carrying into effect not one but all parts of the comprehensive agricultural policy to which the government had committed itself, a plan that would bring that policy out from under the eclipse of parity prices and give the part represented by the FSA equal, if not prior, emphasis. The Farm Bureau Federation had opposed the FSA and wanted to dissolve its successor, the Farmers' Home Administration, in other agencies. The Farmers' Union gave the agency and all it stood for first place on its agenda. The Federation, or, more precisely, some of its state bureaus, and its Associated Women of the American Farm Bureau Federation endorsed family farming as something desirable.[53] The Farmers' Union campaigned for it as something essential. The Federation was content to let the institution share as it might in the profits flowing through the channel of parity prices. The Union would not only dig another channel— of minimum income and wages—but would create new family farms out of units above and below family size. The Federation's main concern was the prosperity of agriculture, the Union's, the welfare of farmers, particularly small farmers. Each favored an administrative system in which it could cut some ice: the Federation, the Extension Service-county agent system; the Union, a system of elective committees of which its official paper declared, "We can put Farmers' Union people on those Committees. We can work in that kind of a setup. We can be more active than anyone else." [54] Both spoke the language of pressure politics, but the Union, withal,

---

53. Resolutions of the Associated Women of the American Farm Bureau Federation at 12th Annual Meeting, December 8-9, 1946. AFBF *Official News Letter*, Dec. 25, 1946, p. 6.
54. *National Union Farmer*, June 1, 1947, p. 3.

presented the most detailed, and, on the whole, the most consistent, plan for carrying the theory of family farming into practice of any political organization.

The Farm Bureau Federation and the Farmers' Union confront us, in the idiom of practical politics, with the alternatives represented respectively by the British experience and the French contrast. It is true that the Extension Service, to whose mast the Federation has nailed its colors, was and is one of the most conscientious supporters of family farming. At its annual convention in 1941, the Association of Land-Grant Colleges' Committee on Citizenship Training reminded the Association that such had been the purpose of the Extension Service from its inception, and recommended as both concept and title for the latter's program, "To Maintain and Preserve for America, the Family Farm." [55] In 1944 the Association's Committee on Postwar Agricultural Policy called for "policies based on panoramic rather than keyhole views of society," specifically the policy of full production and employment to which we have already alluded,[56] and went on record in favor of family farming as follows:

In the first place, the family-type farm should remain the basis on which American agriculture typically is organized. Although there is no reason to standardize all farms, because of differences in agricultural requirements and in the managerial abilities of farmers, the best interest of the country will be served when a majority of farms are of a type on which the operator, with the help of his family and perhaps a moderate amount of outside labor, can make a satisfactory living and maintain the farm's productivity and assets.[57]

This was precisely the policy in favor in official circles and among economists generally. The Committee's definition of a family farm was practically identical with the one approved

55. Association of Land-Grant Colleges and Universities, 55th Annual Convention, Chicago, Ill., Nov. 10-12, 1941, *Proceedings*, p. 198.
56. Cf. p. 157, text and n. 67 above.
57. *Postwar Agricultural Policy*, p. 30.

by the Department of Agriculture in 1945.[58] Such statements
on the part of the intellectual leaders of the administrative
system to which the Farm Bureau Federation wished to en-
trust all agricultural policy show that both attached more
importance to family farming than did the British. Generally speaking, however, the Federation inclined toward the
British view of agriculture as a productive enterprise in which
whatever size or type of farm proved most efficient was desirable.

The president of the Farmers' Union, for his part, denied
"categorically" that he wanted to "keep everybody on the
farm." He said he was just as anxious as anybody to arrive
at a national maximum of production and employment and
an optimum allocation of labor resources between agriculture and industry. Nevertheless, he favored positive measures to ensure that all who remained in agriculture did so
as family farmers, and his proposed minimum income guarantee tended to lessen the incentive to move out.[59] He repeated the maxim that family farming was the "final stronghold" against tyranny and oppression; [60] and if his plan included *remembrement* and a better allocation of labor resources between agriculture and industry, it was just enough
more interested in small farms and agriculture as a way of
life to make it French in spirit rather than British.

But the prospects for family farming and the political
theory that supports it involve much more than a choice between parties and pressure groups. The parties honor each
other by imitation. The pressure groups blur the issue in
their struggle for power. Left to their own devices, farmers
might never settle it. Their agrarian fundamentalism, which
is supposed to have its corollary in democratic fundamen-

58. Cf. p. 134 above.
59. *Hearings on Long-Range Policy*, p. 173. For full testimony on
    this point, pp. 171-174.
60. Cf. p. 199 above.

talism, is not fundamental enough to unite them in practical politics. Their most powerful, and, in the sense of having the greatest influence on public policy, their most representative, political organization has given lip service to the theory; but in practice it has countenanced, and even abetted, a situation that is a long way from either a democratic or an economic optimum and in which family farming is making heavy weather. Their most militant champion of the theory is the smallest of their political organizations, lacking in itself the strength it needs to achieve its goals. Unable to amass that strength in its own, agrarian constituency, it is trying to recruit it outside through alliance with organized labor. Is there any better proof that agriculture by itself is no wonder-working democratic Providence?

We can expect no democratic miracles from agriculture or any other particular part of our economy. We can expect them only from democracy itself. No other force is likely to control and direct the "sweep of mechanization" toward democratic ends, in farming, in business, in manufacturing, or in any other field of enterprise. The only sure source of democracy in any of these is a national wellspring that feeds all of them, not just a source among farmers, or, as we should say, among some farmers. The lesson is plain in history. Family farming cannot save democracy. Only democracy can save the family farm.

It is sometimes thought that the latter has found its salvation, and with it, perhaps, the salvation of democracy, in the co-operative movement. That, too, stands in need of democratic guidance. Supported by both parties, all three major pressure groups, and the government,[61] the co-operative movement has grown to such proportions that in 1946 it included 10,150 farmers' marketing and purchasing asso-

61. Through the Capper-Volstead Law (1922), authorizing processing and marketing co-operatives to operate in interstate commerce; the

ciations with a total membership of 4,505,000 and an annual business of $5,645,000,000.[62] On the face of it there was no more encouraging sign of the good estate of democracy and free enterprise. All over western Europe, particularly in the Scandinavian countries, co-operatives have proved a boon to small-scale purchasers and producers, and to this rule our farmer co-operatives have been no exception.

Neither have they been immune to the tendencies that have affected ordinary business. We have noted Marx's opinion of co-operatives as a fulfillment of capitalism rather than as a reform or corrective.[63] In certain respects it is justified. Starting nearly always as purchasing devices whereby the farmer sought to protect himself as a consumer, they nearly always move on into the field of selling and end by representing the farmer as a producer. The next step is from small to big business. We have already discovered several co-operative associations and the National Council of Farmer Co-operatives among the most active and influential lobbyists for commodity price subsidies in Washington.[64] In the nineteen-twenties cotton co-operatives all over the country united in an avowed, if futile, crusade to monopolize the cotton market.[65] A more recent instance of the same sort was afforded in January, 1947, when the Dairymen's League Co-operative Association, representing 900 local dairy co-

Revenue Acts of 1926 and 1934 exempting them from income, capital gains, and excess profits taxes; and the Co-operative Research and Service Division and the banks for co-operatives of the Farm Credit Administration, to cite the principal measures.

62. *The 13th Annual Report of the Farm Credit Administration*, 1947, pp. 118-119.
63. Cf. pp. 120-121 above.
64. Cf. p. 187 above.
65. This and other details of the co-operative movement from Elsworth, R. H., *The Story of Farmers' Cooperatives*, Farm Credit Administration, 1939; Cowling, Ellis, *Co-operatives in America*, New York, 1943; Landis, Benson Y., *A Cooperative Economy*,

operatives in New York, Pennsylvania, New Jersey, and New England and a volume of business second only to the two largest dairy products corporations,[66] pleaded guilty in the New York Federal District Court to charges of manipulating the wholesale price of butter in violation of the Commodities Exchange Act.[67]

At the time, the supply of dairy products exceeded the demand in eastern markets. To prevent this from lowering current market prices, and with them the next month's parity prices based on them, the League spent over $500,000 and bought up 97 per cent of the butter sold in these markets during the week before Christmas, 1946. It may have been, and undoubtedly was, acting in the supposed interests of its members as producers, but the New York City Consumers Council found its tactics indistinguishable from those of any ordinary monopoly. In the entire co-operative movement its tactics were exceptional, but not its size, its organization, or its philosophy. These were typical of many co-operatives,[68] and, what is more to the point, they were also typical of big business. That co-operatives favor small, individual enterprise is by no means axiomatic of their mere existence. They, too, are part of a greater whole.

For democracy to save the family farm, those who believe in the latter must find in it more than a romantic symbol

New York, 1943; and Roohan, James E., *Cooperation Among American Farmers*, unpublished ms., Yale University Graduate School, 1947.

66. National Dairy Products and Borden. Hoffman, A. C., *Large-Scale Organization in the Food Industries*, TNEC Monograph No. 35, pp. 30 ff.

67. Roohan, *op. cit.*, pp. 1, 42-50; New York *Times*, Jan. 5, 8, 28, 1947.

68. E.g., Land O'Lakes Creameries, National Livestock Producers Association, California Fruit Growers' Exchange, National Cooperative Milk Producers' Federation, American Cotton Co-operative Association, The National Wool Marketing Corporation, etc.

or tradition. The romance and symbolism have played their part, and just about played it out. They have inspired and helped to sustain an eleventh-hour determination to "do something for agriculture," but they have not, and cannot, carry that determination to constructive practical conclusions. On the contrary, they are being denounced by reformers for concealing realities and hampering, rather than furthering, their aims. By the same token we must find in the family farm more than the tradition of laissez-faire government. All parties have rejected this in favor of public price subsidies and marketing and production controls. Even the critics of parity concede the wisdom of government "intervention" for purposes of education, trade regulation, economic planning and, above all, for conservation of the soil.

Nor is the family farm sacred as private property. Generally speaking, private property is as popular with the human race as it ever was: witness the efforts of all who have it to keep it and the efforts of all who do not have it to obtain it; the efforts of all conservative parties to defend it and the efforts of all liberal and radical parties to widen its distribution. Generally speaking, modern productive techniques have brought it nearer than ever to universal possession and enjoyment. But this is not true of all kinds of private property, and it is particularly not true of private property in land. Every country has its man-land ratio, whatever its political philosophy. Though ours does not approach the ratios of Europe and Asia, or of the two democracies whose land policies we have compared with our own, nevertheless our agricultural land is relatively scarce, expensive, and difficult to own, compared to what it was in Jefferson's time. The increase in our population and the development of an industrialized, commercial economy, as Locke and Jefferson both foresaw, have bid up its value until it has become unattainable to many farmers and undesirable to others—too scarce and expensive, at all events, for its possession to be considered a *sine qua non* of democracy.

Though the statistics by themselves do not show it, the fact is that many farmers prefer to lease their farms and invest the capital thus saved in production. Many find greater security in leases than in mortgages. This British heresy together with the practical impossibility of eliminating so high an incidence of tenancy altogether, has led modern agricultural economists to think better of it than politicians do, and to ask for improvements in the form of leases and in the general relations of landlords to tenants as an alternative to fee-simple ownership.[69] In political theory this means that agricultural leaseholds are not necessarily incompatible with democracy. This pragmatic attitude toward private property in land is consistent with the utilitarian concept that has superseded the concept of natural rights. No one any longer believes property to be a natural right. In due course even Jefferson had doubts about it, declaring it was "a moot question whether the origin of any kind of property is derived from nature at all. . . ."[70] Everywhere the possession and use of private property, both in kind and in amount, have been qualified by considerations of the public interest. Russia has nationalized her land and Great Britain has all but followed suit.[71] Private ownership of American family farms is still

69. This was a policy of the FSA, over 70 per cent of whose clients were tenants. Cf. *Toward Farm Security*, p. 78; also Tolley, H. R., "Some Essentials of a Good Agricultural Policy," *1940 Yearbook*, p. 1181; Salter, Leonard A., Jr., "Farm Property and Agricultural Policy," *Journal of Political Economy*, 1943, Vol. LI, pp. 13-22; Assn. of Land-Grant Colleges and Universities, *Postwar Agricultural Policy*, pp. 30 ff.

70. Jefferson to Isaac McPherson, August 13, 1813. Text from Padover, S. K., *The Complete Jefferson*, New York, 1943, p. 1015.

71. With the Agriculture Bill of 1946, making all farms that fail to measure up to standards of production and management prescribed

held desirable—"a large proportion of farms should be owned by those who operate them, and a continuing stream of those who engage in farming should eventually become owners" [72]—but the acceptance on equal terms of the written leasehold protected by public law means that it is no longer deemed essential, even in principle. For these reasons it is unlikely that family farming will be saved because it is sacred to the property right.

Its strongest claim on democracy, the one by which it will either stand or fall as democratic political theory, is this: for all its corruption by industry, business, and government, it is still the outstanding form of individual economic enterprise. For all the 40 per cent of our agricultural land in farms of 1,000 acres and over, the overwhelming majority, even of the top third of our farms that produce 80 per cent of our market requirements, are small-scale family or family-type units; and for all the concentration of control in the food industries, the farmer's market is more competitive than that of other producers. [73] A family farm of the type and dimensions

by the Ministry of Agriculture and Fisheries subject to confiscation by forced sale, and the Town and Country Planning Bill of 1947, virtually nationalizing the use of, and profits from, all urban and suburban land. See Great Britain, Ministry of Agriculture and Fisheries, Agriculture Bill—Explanatory Memorandum Cmd. 6996, London, Dec. 1946, and Minister of Town and Country Planning, Explanatory Memorandum Cmd. 7006, London, Jan., 1947.

72. *Postwar Agricultural Policy*, p. 30.

73. The three highest percentages of total business controlled by the three leading firms in the food industries as compared with other industries, as reported by the TNEC, were:

Food		*Others*	
Meat packing	43	Automobile manufacturing	90
Dairy products	42.6	Farm machinery	84
Flour milling	38	Cigarette manufacturing	80

Hoffman, A. C., *Large-Scale Organization in the Food Industries*, TNEC Monograph No. 35, p. 90. Cf. Blaisdell, TNEC No. 26, p. 175.

stipulated by our theory—one "on which the operator, with the help of his family and perhaps a moderate amount of outside labor, can make a satisfactory living and maintain the farm's productivity and assets" [74]—affords scope for a citizen to live and work more or less on his own terms, to develop the initiative and resourcefulness, the sense of responsibility and the self-respect that have always and everywhere been considered among the greatest assets of democracy. If we still count them as such, not symbolically, but concretely and instrumentally, like our physical resources and our geographical position, we will support family farming as we will all socially constructive individual enterprise. The question is, do we really believe in free enterprise in these vital terms?

We say so, in all our state papers, on every possible occasion—the latest in point being the Economic Report of the President, of February, 1947. But do we mean it? Since 1890 monopoly has been against the law in the United States, yet in 1935 the Bureau of Internal Revenue reported that of all corporations reporting from every part of the nation, one-tenth of 1 per cent of them owned 52 per cent of the assets of all of them; less than 5 per cent owned 87 per cent of the assets of all; and one-tenth of 1 per cent earned 50 per cent, and less than 4 per cent earned 84 per cent, of their total net income.[75] It was on the strength of these figures that Franklin D. Roosevelt launched the most thoroughgoing investigation of the concentration of economic power in our history and called for an anti-trust program "whose basic thesis is not that the system of free private enterprise for profit has failed in this generation, but that it has not yet been tried." [76] The

74. Cf. p. 134 above.
75. Temporary National Economic Committee, *Final Report and Recommendations*, 77th Cong., 1st Sess., Senate Doc. No. 35, p. 11.
76. Message to Congress, April 29, 1938. *Ibid.*, p. 20.

program was no more than started when the war intervened. The results of the war may be judged from the fact that in 1947 the Monopoly Subcommittee of the House of Representatives Committee on Small Business found that 250 corporations owned or held options to purchase 65 per cent of the total manufacturing facilities of the United States,[77] and from the further fact that, in spite of all the pious resolutions, this Committee was barely able to persuade Congress to renew its appropriations for another year.

If this performance is a measure of our faith in free individual enterprise, the outlook for family farming is black, and the outlook for democracy as we have known and understood it in the past is not much brighter. Agriculture is too susceptible to trends in the rest of the economy to be immune to these. We cannot hope to preserve free enterprise in farming if we do not preserve it elsewhere. Even if we could and the hope were realized, we would have no more than an escapist enclave of dwindling political significance. We could never expect it to exert much influence on unrestrained imperialism in business, industry, and organized labor. We could only expect it to do what it already shows signs of doing: to take the cue of the Farm Bureau Federation's cartoonist as a "powerful organized group competing for economic advantage."

There is a widespread tendency to accept these trends as the inevitable dispensation of technology. To those who hold this view the latest report of the Secretary of Agriculture reads like a vision of apocalypse, a vision of tractors, combines, milking machines, mechanical corn-, cotton- and potato-pickers, pickup balers, harvesters, and loaders over-

77. *United States versus Economic Concentration and Monopoly*, Staff Report to the Monopoly Subcommittee of the Committee on Small Business, House of Representatives, 79th Cong., December 27, 1946, p. 136.

whelming the last outposts of individual enterprise.[78] There can be no doubt that our farmers are caught in the tide of the industrial revolution, which is still at the flood and against which there is no turning back. "Nobody expects farmers to discard their machinery," Secretary Anderson told the Committee on Long-Range Agricultural Policy in 1947—"they show unmistakable signs of doing the opposite."

They are buying improved equipment and as much more of it as they can get. Nobody expects farmers to stop using the crops and practices that produce more per acre at less cost per unit. Nobody expects research men and the engineer to reach the limit of new discoveries and new applications of knowledge. Far from seeing the limit of our productive efficiency, we are just beginning to see the possibilities.[79]

What chance has family farming on this horizon? What price free enterprise of any kind?

Against this view, which has at least as much fatalism in it as it has empirical evidence, is opposed another view, supported by no less impressive evidence. This is the view that economic concentration is caused not so much by technology as by pecuniary profit, opportunism, the thirst for power— human motives, subject to political discipline and control and by no means uniformly profitable when carried to an extreme. In fact, mass production in industry appears to be subject to the same law of diminishing returns as applies to agriculture. After the productive unit has attained a certain size and massiveness, its profits begin to diminish in proportion to the capital invested and the cost of production. In both farming and manufacturing, therefore, the economic optimum is not necessarily represented by the largest units.[80]

78. *Report of the Secretary of Agriculture*, 1946, pp. 48-49.
79. *Hearings on Long-Range Agricultural Policy*, p. 5.
80. For full discussion of this point of view, see Federal Trade Commission, *Relative Efficiency of Large, Medium-Sized, and Small Business*, TNEC Monograph No. 13, Washington, 1941, *passim*, and esp. pp. 405-415.

But this is not the only rift in the clouds. There are signs that industry may come to the rescue of family farming of its own accord, that the mass production of small, versatile, low-cost units may prove as profitable in farm machinery as it has in automobiles.[81] The head of one of the oldest and largest farm machinery firms has predicted that post-war advances in farm technology will "give the small one-family farm every advantage available through mechanical equipment to the larger farm." [82] Rural electrification, progressing rapidly under the Rural Electrification Administration, is providing another hitherto unavailable means of production to small farmers. Co-operative ownership and use may do the same for such agricultural machinery as may be incapable of production in small units. Even in the existing circumstances, the census shows the nation-wide persistence of family farming; and economic studies of family farms of different types and in different regions show a wide variety of conditions—climate, soil, geography, population, type of crop produced, and last but not least, the personal skill and character of the farmer—in which family farming flourishes in competition with large-scale commercial farming.[83]

81. Cf. *Agriculture and the National Economy*, TNEC Monograph No. 23, p. 13.
82. Quoted from testimony before the *Special Committee on Postwar Economic Policy and Planning*, House, 78th Cong., 2nd Sess., Part 5, Dec., 1944, by Liss, Samuel, "Family Farm Perspectives," *Land Policy Review*, Spring, 1947, Vol. X, p. 7.
83. See, for example, Brewster, John M., "Farm Technological Advance and Population Growth," *Journal of Farm Economics*, 1945, Vol. XXVII, pp. 509-525; Johnson, O. R., "The Family Farm," *ibid.*, 1944, Vol. XXVI, pp. 529-548; USDA, Bureau of Agricultural Economics, *Typical Family-Operated Farms, 1930-45: Adjustments, Costs and Returns* (F.M. 55), and *Typical Family-Operated Farms, 1930-45: An Historical Look to the Future* (F.M. 56), Washington, 1946; also the special studies of California farming communities conducted and reported by Goldschmidt, W., *As You Sow*, New York, 1947.

It is a conservative conclusion to draw from this evidence that family farming as we now define it is not doomed by technology. Its economic case is not so hopeless that we cannot save it if we want to. The question is, do we want to? This is not a question of knowing what to do, but of having the will to do it. We know what to do. Our economists have told us, with remarkable unanimity and precision. The historical experiences of England and France, made relevant to us by the common denominator of democracy, bear them out. We know that family farming cannot thrive on the terms of hillbillies and Okies any more than it can amid factories in the field. We know that our goal requires the re-employment of large numbers of farmers and farm laborers in non-agricultural occupations, and a reallocation of productive resources within agriculture in keeping with present and prospective demand rather than with the *status quo* and the political power to defend it. These ends are not promoted by arbitrary rewards in a free-for-all among pressure groups or by a rain of subsidies on the just and the unjust. They are not promoted by agrarian particularism. They can be attained only by a national belief in full production, full employment—and full democracy. Such are the prospects for family farming and democracy in the United States.

Index

Date Due

SEP 21 '53			
MAR 3 '54			
OC 21 '55			
NO 15 '57			
NOV 16			
FEB 24 '61			
MAR 14 '62			
JAN 11 '65			
Demco 293-5			